T0166814

THE
WELLSPRING

'Keep at a tangent.
When they make the circle wide, it's time to swim
out on your own and fill the element
with signatures on your own frequency,
echo soundings, searches, probes, allurements,
elver-gleams in the dark of the whole sea.'

Seamus Heaney, 'Station Island'

THE
WELLSPRING

*Conversations with **David Owen Norris***

BARNEY NORRIS

Seren is the book imprint of
Poetry Wales Press Ltd
57 Nolton Street, Bridgend, Wales, CF31 3AE
www.serenbooks.com
Facebook: facebook.com/SerenBooks
Twitter: @SerenBooks

ISBNs
Hardback – 978-1-78172-464-4
Ebook – 978-1-78172-463-7
Kindle – 978-1-78172-468-2

A CIP record for this title is available from the British Library.

The publisher acknowledges the financial assistance
of the Welsh Books Council.

Printed by TJ International, Cornwall.

Cover artwork: © Dave Evans
www.flickr.com/photos/dave-cool/

Contents

Prologue

An abiding preoccupation with permanence and change, tradition and change, the cycle, the return, is what makes the music of David Owen Norris profound to listen to. The value of its statement lies first of all in the perspective of its composer, whose experience of the world we're in now is focused by a keen awareness of the time that passed before us. In his music, the two are held and considered in relation to one another – not reconciled, but shaped into a chord where both worlds speak together.

This is the work of an Englishman, born in 1953 into a rural village community, whose culture's dissolution represents a profound reimagining of the life of these islands, and who has worked to express that change through music. The roofbeams of Norris' work are what became of the Anglican tradition and its cultural referents: the meat-and-two-veg diet, the long walk, the doffed cap, the quiet life. In the music he makes, Norris hears and documents the passing of a world that has formed and informed us all, the once deafening root note of our culture, now sounding like a river in another valley.

When England was in flood, the England remembered in Norris' work, it told a story about itself calculated to drown any other voices that might have tried to be heard alongside. Its red coated soldiers, its Pomp and Circumstance Marches, its rugby football coalesced into an idea that shaped and governed an extraordinary volume of human activities and decisions, for an extraordinarily long time.

During the course of Norris' lifetime, that image has dissipated, and been replaced by a new and richer plurality. It feels increasingly difficult to remember how the story of England once went – how we could ever have been proud, as a culture, of much that our ancestors seemed to value. We recognise ever more clearly that while the narrative of England was in the ascendant, infinite others were cast into shadow, and went unexplored, and that infinite consequences unfolded from that. Haltingly, we have begun the process of seeking to excavate some of the tracks that were covered over by the river of England when it was in spate.

This does not mean, though, that we should forget the story of England as it's glimpsed in Norris' work. It is a narrative that has organised so much of the history of our culture, and continues to do so. It shapes so many of the decisions we make in our lives. It merits study, if we are to try and understand ourselves. And it is perhaps uniquely interesting to think about this narrative now, when the idea of its primacy is overturned, and it can be seen as one thread of story intertwining endlessly with countless others. It seems particularly interesting to me to be able to examine the memory of England now we think of it as only one of the songs we might choose to sing.

That's what I find compelling in the music of David Owen Norris. He finds ways to ask what this idea of England used to mean, and what it might mean for us now. He documents the disappearance of a world. Crucially, though, he is capable of sufficient ironic detachment from his theme to connect that sensation of disappearance to the hills-old human need to always see the world as ending, our continual conversation with our mortality. So listening to his music leads to much more than simply thinking about England. The countries, towns, streets, houses we live in come to seem incidental when set against the value we place on the lives we lived while we occupied those spaces, and we quickly realise the furniture and scenery of our lives weren't what mattered at all. Places are vessels into which we pour our lives, and though they shape them, they never become them. Our lives are elsewhere. The real reason someone might take an interest in England is because it was where they were young – the place is secondary to that. So Norris' music shows us that to begin to consider the memory of *an* identity – Englishness – is very quickly to begin thinking about the memory of *your own* identity, your unique and personal experience of being in the world – and indeed of *all* identity: the way it gathers together, the way it frays.

Through Norris' preoccupation with his cultural hinterland, he allows his work to speak to more than just the millenarian in each of us, but more meaningfully to the universal experience of death in life and life in death that is at the centre of who we all are. In his work, the ineluctable diminution of the sacredness of Sunday that all of us have lived through since shops changed their opening hours, and everyone stopped getting married in churches, is not treated as a subject in itself, but as a window into thinking about our real lives. He is able to remind us that the world is always ending; even within the fast-bound unit of a family, each successive generation is a unique iteration, never to be repeated, a pattern almost immediately sublimated back into the endless, Darwinian delta of life as it flows through time. In Norris' work we are reminded that everything you ever put your finger on is always being subsumed into something else, like patterns in clouds or shapes in a coal fire, even as you try to treat it as a constant, as fixed: the only thing that's permanent is change.

Across the distance of this perspective, Norris' elegies for his own hinterland are transmuted into acts of celebratory commemoration. He is able to envisage not only a continuation but also an expansion of the essential, underlying meaning of his cultural inheritance even as it disappears, as it is absorbed into new forms, new worlds, new societies. So the evocation of that inheritance in his music becomes a powerful social action, as listeners are reminded who they are – or rather, of some of the places they came from. In its style, its interests, its stances, all of which place him outside the main stream of our contemporary culture, among gestures which could be termed anachronistic but which I choose to read as a deliberate curation of source material, his output takes the form of music played for vanished and departed listeners, for a world that no longer exists. But he spins his yarns out of these anachronisms because the act of playing re-members those listeners, re-integrates them into our present social discourse, and bequeaths a sense of the timelessness and endlessness of all human hopes and fears to our now, through the coal-fire shapes the singing takes. His work is what it sounds like to love our history from the vantage of the present, and this, for me, is an urgent moral project: it might be that by cultivating that sound, new routes could be opened into a richer relationship for all of us with the cacophony of the self.

*

David Owen Norris is my father. I don't know an enormous amount about my parents' lives before I was part of them – I don't think I've ever seen a photo of their wedding – but the facts as I understand them are that for a while after their marriage they lived in Harlesden until Dad got an organist job in Sussex that came with a cottage. I was born a little while after they moved there, and my brother was born a couple of years later. The cottage wasn't really big enough for four of us, so the Earl of Egremont, who attended the church where Dad played, let us move into one of his hunting lodges. We lived there for a couple of years, looking out over a wheat field, hidden in the woods, and then Dad won a major award in the US. At this point we moved into a rented farmhouse, which has subsequently become the lost domain which I have sought to dream my way back to ever since.

The award was good news for the career and the bank balance, but it put an intolerable pressure on my parents' marriage. Dad spent much of the year on tour in America, and Mum found herself alone in the country with two small children. They divorced when I was six. Dad moved back to Harlesden. Mum bought a house in Putney, and we went to live with Mum, later making our way further west to Wiltshire, which became home, the site of my second childhood, that took the place of my first life in Sussex, which ended when my parents divorced.

I share all this because it seems to me to be fundamental to the writing of this book. Any child who grows up with an absent parent will come to be preoccupied with roots and with inheritance. A child who spends time living in someone's spare hunting lodge, in the dreamlike environment of Sussex in the late 80s and early 90s, will be doubly aware of the way their background forms them, by virtue of looking at things through very different eyes to others. I have always felt the route I took into life encased me in a kind of difference from the people I grew up around. It's not just the obvious things – it's true that my environment was completely white, and I think the only non-white faces I'd ever seen before we moved to London were pictures of Fats Waller and the Inkspots on the front of cassettes, all of which made me conscious of difference and interested in difference, when we moved to London and I learned how big the world was.

There were also other, stranger differences, quirks of the culture I was born into. I'm thinking of the fact that I never encountered football when I was in Sussex. We played marbles in the playground. We read the *Children's Illustrated Bible*. There were also differences which came about as a result of geography. I know things about hedgerows that other people, particularly those of my age or younger, are unlikely to know. I have seen glow worms and held shrews in my palm, captured crickets in jam jars and stumbled on adders, shocked sleeping does and buzzards into flight. These aren't things the majority of people are exposed to any more. I have always felt in my day-to-day life that I reach people through layer on layer of silence and woodland and solitude, and I've always suspected that the first views revealed to me formed the way I see everything else.

To be clear, what this taught me wasn't that I was different from other people. I learned instead that everyone is different from other people. We all carry within us a private world, our histories, which govern and shape our lives even as we live them. Ever since I discovered this truth for myself, the idea of mapping those worlds and the conversations they have with the present has been important to me.

It was thinking about my relationship with my Dad that led me to a serious consideration of these ideas, and perhaps that was the start of wanting to write this book. Until I was near the end of my school years, I never thought about the fact that my parents had divorced. It was a fact of life, and I was happy, and I had a happy childhood. But a time came when I became aware it must have made a difference, never to have said 'Mum' and 'Dad' in the same sentence; things must inevitably have been different from how they were first planned to be. This was the question that set me to writing. My first play was called *Regrets*, and it was about a son refusing to inherit what his parents had left for him. It was performed for a single night in the Salberg Studio at Salisbury Playhouse, and the script is mercifully lost. My second play, also mercifully lost, was a monologue I performed myself, called *Twice As Many Christmas Presents*. It was even worse than it sounds. Still, it was the start of something, and the attempt to understand the influences which formed me has subsequently grown into a life.

As I was leaving school, I began to imagine an absence where my understanding of my father might have been, a distance between us that hadn't been filled by quotidian experience, because our relationship had always been structured around holidays and weekends. An undiscovered country, demanding exploration.

*

In 2015, I was appointed as the Martin Esslin Playwright in Residence at Keble College, Oxford, a return to the place where I spent my undergraduate years. Roger Boden, the college bursar, had brought the role into being as a way for me to re-engage with the place where I first formed my opinions. I took up the position because I was looking for new thinking to feed my work, and wanted to go back to the wellspring. When I was at Keble the first time round, I'd made a five year plan for breaking into the theatre. Since graduating I'd followed it precisely, and the plan had worked. Having completed it, I wanted to come up with another plan. I like playing the long game. So I went back to Keble to develop a new strategy for saying what I wanted to say in the way that I wanted to say it.

One of the things I found myself thinking about upon my return was my relationship with my father. Dad had gone to Keble before me, and is now an honorary fellow of the college. Keble had become a central element of his identity, as it is of mine. From the start of my relationship with the place, I had engaged with it as a sideways attempt to get closer to my father. Back when I first applied to study at Oxford, I was saddled with AS Level results that were somewhat depressed by a weed habit, and didn't look like much of a candidate. I almost didn't bother applying because success seemed so unlikely, but stuck my hat in the ring on an impulse, on the day applications closed, because if you don't try, you never know, do you? I applied specifically to Keble because it was the only college I really knew, and because I thought Dad might be pleased. I got an offer, and stopped taking drugs, and got the grades I needed. Then Dad was driving me up and I was unpacking my books into a room there.

Throughout my undergraduate years at Keble, I maintained a curious shadow relationship with Dad, in addition to the actual relationship between us that continued when I came home in the holidays (from the age of nineteen to the age of twenty-seven I lived intermittently in Dad's spare room, whenever I didn't have money). As well as having my own experience of Keble, I was aware of my life as a palimpsest of his. I knew I was in his footsteps, and seeing things he had seen when he was my age. It was a curious thing, having felt distant from my father, to suddenly feel so close, to the point where the very idea of my individuality was a little subsumed – I was simply a reformulation of something that had previously been him, walking the same streets with a few variables (time, 50% of my DNA) thrown in. I thought a great deal about this strange idea of the individual life as palimpsest. To see different generations of a family as successive iterations of a continuous, continuing experience was captivating to me. What was this larger life we were part of, this family? How were the unique experiences of different generations inherited by that continuing river, and what was lost with each life as it passed? What would be seen to be constant, and what would be seen to change, if we could only glimpse for a moment the perspective of that whole family, and break out of the cells of ourselves?

Coming back to Keble brought me back to these questions, and this book is the result of trying to engage with them. I hope that by engaging with the work of my father, I will perhaps light upon a fruitfully oblique approach to the preoccupations that work prompted in me. The book is also, of course, a slantwise look at Dad's music, and I hope its publication might encourage further studies by writers more musicologically articulate than myself. For now, though, I propose to take a walk through the woods of the fact that life happens and then ends, and that we spend our lives trying to get our heads around those two vast inevitabilities, in the company of my Dad.

Listening

BN: Perhaps one of the propositions woven into the fabric of this book is that in order to begin to understand someone, you have to understand where they came from, the place where the river rises. Could you begin by telling me a little of your own family?

DON: My father Bert and I were born in the same village in the wilds of Northamptonshire, 33 years apart. My grandfather (an incomer from Crick) had been Long Buckby Co-Op's farm manager – they said he had the loudest voice in the village, calling the cows home for milking. Dad was very much the baby of the family: my grandfather had five children by his first wife, who died in 1900, and then three more by his second wife. At this point, the Great War took away three of his sons, and so, possibly from motives almost of economic prudence, my father was born in 1920.

BN: He had a lot of older nephews and nieces who used to push 'uncle Bertie' round in his pram.

DON: Indeed. And isn't that image interesting? There's something arresting, I think, in the idea of a younger uncle. Mended mirrors spring to mind – the shards not fitting back together quite right. The legacy of the Great War.

Once out of the pram, Dad passed the exam for the Grammar School, but his father couldn't afford to send him, so he got a job as a delivery boy for the shoe factory, taking cut-out leather to the hand-sewn men, who worked at home.

BN: This is very good social history, this detail, and we should record it. As I understand it, when big shoe factories were first going up in Northampton, the skilled workers were still sufficiently powerful to get away with refusing to be centralised. They all had their set-ups at home, their worksheds at the bottom of the garden, and they didn't want to commute into work, they liked their lives at home well enough. So the compromise reached was that the leather would be cut out in a big factory building, then shipped out to where these men lived and worked, and the shoes brought back to be buffed when they were finished. That was Grandad's job, he was a runner, wasn't he.

DON: But only for as long as he had to be. In 1938 he joined the Navy, and soon after war broke out he was seconded to what was left of the French Navy.

BN: More or less by accident.

DON: He'd been on a ship that hit a mine in Scapa Flow, then he'd been on shore leave from the *Hood* on the day it was sunk. Both of these were terrible events, and he wanted a change, so he volunteered for submarine duty. But when you volunteered for special service you didn't necessarily get the special service you asked for, and that was how he found his way into the Free French. This brought him the Croix de Guerre and a minute pension from the French Government: he was much prouder of the latter than the former. Being bombed at Narvik and then sailing round the world pretty well slaked Dad's desire for travel, and the year before I was born, he and my mother planned out the house where I was born in Buckby.

BN: They had this house built in 1952, and went on to live in it.

DON: It was very difficult to get Dad to leave it ever afterwards, though he earned his living by driving round the country selling nuts and bolts. He did this until his company took the fatal decision to sell as many as they could make, rather than to make as many as they could sell. He spent his very lengthy retirement (getting on forty years) as a superbly accomplished amateur carpenter.

The war was, of course, the central event of his life, as it was with all his generation. At the end of his life, when he was in hospital, he told the story time and again of passing a ship at sea, and signalling 'hello' to the signalman on the other deck, then watching as a bomb hit that deck, and the other signalman vanished forever in the carnage. He was transfixed by that memory, he couldn't get away from it. But life became very vivid for people in that period.

Some of the stories he told us are really extraordinary. In Scapa Flow, where the ship he was on was holed by a mine, he told us the ship's lieutenant gambled on the fact it was a magnetic mine had done the damage, and any others lying round wouldn't latch onto a dinghy. So this lieutenant detailed a man named Pookie Finn to row him to shore in a dinghy he thought wouldn't attract any further mines. Of course, the very first thing that happened was that the dinghy hit another mine, and Dad watched as Pookie Finn was shot a hundred feet into the air. Then he claimed to have seen a man shot in the head for queue-jumping in Malaysia. And he claimed to have lost the entire French fleet while he was signalman on the *Emile Bertin*. And all of this pales into insignificance, of course, when set against the months he apparently spent living in a village in the Congo, after the ship he was serving on had sunk and he had made it to shore. He claimed to have stayed in this village till an attempt was made to marry him off to a local girl, at which point he said he swapped his leather jacket for a coracle and paddled back out to the nearest passing ship.

BN: I told that story to a retired brigadier-general I met not so long ago, and his response made it very clear that Grandad would have had some fast talking to do after that one, it was almost certainly worth a court martial.

DON: Yes, but he seems to have got away with it! Which may, of course, lend the lie to that rather tall tale, but that's by the by.

BN: Yes, the story's the thing. I was delighted to read Sebastian Barry saying in an interview not so long ago that he quite liked it when his interlinking novels and plays contradicted one another on certain particulars, because that's what storytelling's like. A lovely way to approach things.

And what of the other side of your family?

DON: My mother, Margaret, who was universally known as Peggy, was born in a tiny village suburb of nearby Daventry, and attended the Grammar School that Dad so conspicuously didn't – as in turn did my elder brother John and I. Her father had left Snowdonia when his farm was dug up by the slate company, and by 1910 he was driving a London bus. He served in Mesopotamia in the Great War, then worked his way back along the Watling Street in the direction of Wales till he met my grandmother and got stuck in Northamptonshire.

My Mum and Dad met on and off for several years, and eventually got married on Christmas Day 1942 – Dad had a day's leave.

BN: The story as I had it from Grandma was that after her Dad came out of the army he tried to run a taxi for a while, but wasn't a great timekeeper and never managed to meet the train, which was the main source of passengers. Then someone who had known his family back in Wales, who was doing all right for themselves as a farmer, gave him a job as a chauffeur, because this bloke owned two Daimlers that he liked to go around in. So your grandfather worked as a farmhand and a driver, and had use of the Daimlers, so Grandma claims, when they weren't needed. Which was probably highly useful when it came to courting!

DON: That was the connection that got him up to Daventry, yes, but more than anything else it was the farm work that was the centre of his life. And he was the keeper on a golf course as well, because it was below the cottage where they lived. Mum would have to take a long stick out with her on the way to school, and knock the worm casts off the greens. Her Dad would spend his day among cattle. They had a churning bowl in the cellar below the cottage. A big stone open bowl, and you churned the butter yourself. Mice would fall in.

BN: Then I think it's worth telling the story of your parents' wedding.

DON: It's a good story. As I say, Dad had a day's leave. The night before the wedding he got the train back, then walked the last ten miles home, and had a bowl of rice pudding to eat that was meant for the dogs the next morning. The next day was the wedding, and then there was a breakfast where they were thirteen at table and shared a bottle of sherry between them. During the course of the day the news came on the radio that servicemen were getting an extra day's leave, and just had to report to their embarkation points, which was the railway station for Dad, to confirm they hadn't gone AWOL. So the next morning a friend who was a taxi driver gave Mum and Dad a lift part of the way back to the station to do this and claim their extra day, but his petrol ration ran out half way, so they walked the last four miles together. Then they arrived at the station to be told the extra day's leave didn't apply to the Navy, and Dad had to head back there and then. So they said goodbye to each other on the platform, and Dad had to get on the train. Two years passed before they saw one another again.

BN: When they do meet again it always seems to be in Glasgow or London, doesn't it, Grandad back on flying visits to wherever Grandma was working as a Secretary for the War Office. I find it ever so slightly impossible to get a handle on it all.

DON: That's the fog of war, I think.

BN: Quite.

So, onwards. I'm hoping to establish a portrait of your England, your home. What was Long Buckby like when you first knew it, and Northamptonshire?

DON: The Long Buckby of my childhood was a place that has

vanished now, of course, in many respects. I remember the call the women of the village used – 'Oo-ooh', they shrilled across the Market Square, but no longer. The headscarves linger on a bit – every woman wore one when I was little. I spent a great deal of time with my mother's parents, who had retired to Buckby from farming. They had both been Methodists, but they didn't always see eye-to-eye, so on arrival in Buckby, Pap chose the Congregational Chapel, and Nana, the Baptists. The Baptists, in those days, was where you went if you found the Church of England too exciting. Since Mum taught in the village school (where I had to call her Miss), I had my dinners at Nana's. Dinner, in Long Buckby, still just about remains a mid-day meal. Nana used to have her *lunch* (cup of tea and a biscuit) about 11.

Nana believed every word in the Bible, and it wasn't till I was twelve years old that I even began to wonder whether she was quite right about that. She told me tales of her brother, who died at Ypres, and who made up a sort of quartet with the three unknown half-uncles whose names were read out from the war memorial every November, as I stood to attention, a shivering Wolf Cub.

It's very easy to steep yourself in the past where everything and everyone you see and know are part of your family history, as was the case for me, in that village where my father's family had lived for so long. I became intensely attached to What Was, and accordingly I became a diligently conventional child. Many of those conventions have stuck deep within me, so I suspect I appear much less conventional now, not having moved all that much with the current.

BN: Your account raises two points I think worth observing, elements that I think have fallen away from their former ubiquity, and which represent a great change. The first is that Biblical background. That can't be overstated, I think, as a change to the fabric of our country, to think that everyone up to and including the Beatles was pretty much off-book on the Bible, and now, in the course of a lifetime, I'd say its role as a living document in people's lives is very difficult to put a finger on. Not that people haven't always written about the tide of faith receding, and only the elderly worrying about God or whatever, but it really is a profound difference, to see how it's been shunted to the cultural margins.

DON: That is in part your secular perspective, of course. In communities up and down Britain, faith is still central to life, even while it has ceased to resonate in other places.

BN: You're absolutely right – but I was fascinated to read recently that the only time Thatcher ever suffered a defeat in the Commons was over the Shops Bill, in the year of my birth, 1987. This was her attempt to introduce Sunday trading, and she was seen off by a rebellion from Christian backbenchers. The idea of that vote not passing seems very outlandish from where we're standing, and indeed the idea of that lobby having that power again is quite difficult to imagine.

DON: Difficult for now, yes. Productivity is all!

BN: Which is just a different religion, of course.

The second thing to point out is that sense of rootedness in a single place, and that close acquaintance with 'What Was' that you refer to. This is much diminished, I think, by the impact of the Second World War on the country. The New Towns project that happened in the wake of the Blitz, the building of large new urban conurbations to rehome the displaced, means great swathes of the country live in towns some distance from the places where their relatives are buried – where their older history resides. So that sense of the depth of time you refer to, that's much disrupted for many people. As it is by increased social mobility – by people who move away, and go after opportunities. The twentieth century really disrupted the geographical continuity of families in those respects, and the long term consequences of that – which is pretty much a historically unique event, I think – are only just beginning to be felt.

DON: That's certainly hitting home in our family. The nature of my work, and yours, have meant that in our respective twenties, both of us were obliged to move to the capital. For me, having never found my way back to living in Northamptonshire, that means it's difficult to see as much of my brother as I'd naturally want to.

BN: Which is the same with me, and is perhaps why this undertone of exile is creeping into what I have to say about the England you come from, I don't know. I think that geographical dislocation, leading to dislocations within families, is why memories seem so strangely short in modern families as well. I think it's quite remarkable, today, to hear an anecdote dating back more than a couple of generations from anyone. And when you think about it, that's very odd – there's no real reason we don't all carry stocks of much older stories about our families in our heads, except that families haven't spent enough time sat together remembering and talking for the last little while.

Now, I shouldn't make too sweeping a claim for you as any kind of representative example of English cultural hinterland, because that would be a rather exposed promontory on which to place anyone. But I do think any given person has reasonable grounds for being a valid study in such a context, and in your work, it seems to me you've made a concerted and fruitful engagement with the ineluctable nature of cultural change, the way things vanish and the way things remain. That's why I first wanted to undertake this project – I think we share an abiding interest in the way the world ends. And I think the fact of our being father and son is going to enrich any dialogue on that subject – questions of cultural inheritance are innate to exchanges between us. At the outset of this enquiry, then, if you're content to discuss your work through the lens I'm proposing, I thought it might be wise to ask you to make a preliminary sketch of the culture you see yourself as coming from? It would be interesting to triangulate a frame of reference from the off.

DON: Well, every state-secondary-school child in Northamptonshire used to be given an Atlas, an illustrated Bible, and a copy of the little blue hymn-book, *Songs of Praise*. My copy of the latter is full of the names of classical composers, inscribed in red felt-tip as a mute protest against the fact that the school bus played Terry Wogan every morning, though nowadays I see the advantages of an intimate knowledge of the Top Tens of the late 60s.

BN: I have yet to develop much gratitude for knowing the chart hits of the 90s. I wonder whether I ever will…

DON: Perhaps Take That or whoever don't quite equate to a diet of the Beatles and the Beach Boys!

On with my catechism. Vicars were influential in Long Buckby. The mediaeval village had no squire, a fact that explains the 'Long' bit of its name, for fleeing villeins (I like to imagine) fetched up at libertarian Buckby and built a house next to the most recent fugitive, all along the main road. The mediaeval names persist – the top end of the village is called Cotton End (properly Coten, of course, the plural of the word for 'cottage'), and the bottom end is Murcott. For that matter, the bridges on the Daventry road are still called the Birdges, but you'll know more about metathesis than I do. Buckby was very proud of its wholly illusory libertarian attitude when I was a child – I myself (as you may wearily recall) still re-tell the story of how 'we' shrugged off Cromwell when he demanded money on his way to Naseby.

There were a number of people who thought they were the squire (invariably calling forth the very Buckby phrase 'Oozy think eeyiz?'), but only one Vicar at a time. Mr. Yeomans restored the church roof by enrolling everyone in the village as a Coppersmith, a penny a day – pennies were called coppers then: and he started the Wolf Cubs. Most important to me was Mr. Courtenay, a Keble man like you and me (back in the 30s), an escapee from Colditz, and a keen country-dancer and clarinettist. I'd been getting involved with the parish church because the organist had encouraged my interest in the organ, and I was baptised at the age of nineteen. Mr. Courtenay's wife played the cello, and her first act on arriving was to set up a chamber music party at the Vicarage, clarinet, cello, and a very elderly Morningside lady, Mrs. Couling, whose father had been President of the Royal Scottish Academy, and who had studied the violin at the Royal College of Music before the Great War – Parry, Vaughan Williams! – and who had played in Donald Francis Tovey's orchestra in Edinburgh. She had married a wandering painter, and her private amusement was to receive visitors in her cottage, sitting beneath her husband's voluptuous nude studies of her. I was the village pianist at this notable music party (Mozart, I recall, and Beethoven), and my whole professional life was presented to me there in embryo, on that one occasion. I became the accompanist to Mrs. Couling's Women's Institute Choir in nearby Flore (I was an honorary member), and from her and from Mr. Courtenay I imbibed a great dose of their pasts. What were the specific lessons, I wonder? A couple of things stick – Jack Courtenay reading out a line from a hymn – 'before thy throne prostrate to lie, and gaze and gaze on thee' – and exclaiming 'I hope it's not like that! Far too boring.' And Mrs. Couling's careful manipulation of a tape-measure metronome, moving her hand so that the tempo was invariably the one she'd already chosen. And her refrain in her lilting Scots 'remember all those things, David, all those things I've shown you.' And in principle, I have remembered, especially the day she took me to a chamber music concert in the Carnegie Hall (the one in Northampton) to hear Daniel Barenboim, Hugh Bean and Jacqueline du Pré playing Beethoven. The actual thing that I remember is that she wept throughout – made a very great impression on me.

The County Music Adviser, Malcolm Tyler, heard that I played the organ, and took over my lessons himself. He was the first professional musician I'd ever met, and I started to realize that I might not need to be a nuclear physicist after all – not that I'd met one of them either. He introduced me to the idiosyncratic musical life of Northampton – it remains idiosyncratic, thankfully, a function of its distance from London, Oxford, Cambridge and Birmingham, an inconveniently great distance for most of its history, allowing it to develop its own ways of doing things – and an early exhilarating experience was hearing Elgar's *Gerontius* live in the ABC Cinema (idiosyncratically enough, in a town of splendid churches).

Malcolm Tyler studied at the Royal Academy of Music, and pulled a string or two so that I could become the first (and possibly the only ever) member of what they called the Intermediate School – essentially a Gap Year before I went to Keble as the Organ Scholar. It was Jack Courtenay's country-dancing, by the way, that swung my Keble interview. Warden Nineham asked me if I had any hobbies, and some musicians don't. But I could do a quick heel-and-toe by the fireplace.

BN: This gap year was something that involved considerable sacrifice and discomfort for you.

DON: Yes. I took a five-pound note to London on the train every Tuesday morning, and that paid for a couple of concerts at the South Bank, food, buses, and my train-ticket back again – I bought the ticket on the way back, not the way out, because it was cheaper to buy a return from London to Buckby, with the weekend intervening. I used to keep accounts on the back of my bus-ticket – Harry Isaacs, my piano teacher, spotted me jotting down the price of a cup of tea, and said grandly 'Ah, my boy, that way madness lies.' I didn't realize it was a quotation. Very bad advice, probably – I've never since been much good at accounts.

The minister at Buckby Baptists had arranged for me to sleep for free on the study floor at Abbey Road Baptist Church. It was not without its perils. One dark night I took a short-cut across the baptistery and only discovered half-way down the steps that it was full of water warming up ready for a baptism the following day. And one fine morning I woke rather later than usual to find my sleeping-bag surrounded by a whole class of trainee missionaries from Sweden.

Occasionally the five-pound note didn't go far enough, and I was really hungry. Once, I'm sorry to say, I raided the Abbey Road kitchen. All they'd left out was plain yoghurt and a raw onion, and I can still taste them. Sometimes, though, there was enough money left to buy an Agatha Christie at Euston – those half-crown editions with cover art by Tom Adams were just coming out. As soon as I got back to Buckby, I leapt into the car to take a choir-practice in a nearby village for one of the many musical vicars in my life, the one who thought that every family sang madrigals as a matter of course. The madrigal books came out with the coffee mugs whenever anyone visited the vicarage.

I spent the weekends practising, of course, since my London days were pretty full with my own lessons, accompanying other people's lessons, and going to concerts. All in all it was a strenuous year. Astonishingly good value at £5 a week.

BN: I remember reading somewhere in Martin Amis's *The War Against Cliché* that the cost of things when he was making his way into writing – slightly before your time, of course – meant that the idea of a 'life in letters' was so much more accessible than it is to people now. A reviewing gig might cover the rent. You come across it in David Hare's memoir *The Blue Touch Paper* – he was very successful very early, so he's not a model you can really extrapolate from, but all the same, I can't believe the equivalent level of success today would make it possible to live in the post codes he did. Things just cost less then. There was a moment, wasn't there, of great possibility for movement and achievement and change, because education had improved so rapidly, and the cost of things was still low, relative to today.

DON: There was a feeling of endless possibility, if you could take what was on offer. Some of our ideas were perhaps a bit simplistic. I remember Mum and Dad made it sound like I'd be able to do literally anything I liked with my life, if I passed the eleven plus. That exam is a greater divider of opinion now than it was then, so we won't get lost in the thickets of 'if there were more grammar schools they wouldn't be the preserve of those who can afford to move to the towns that kept them going', or its counter-argument; let's just note that in those days, grammar selection was by no means all along lines of class or parental income. In parenthesis, Philip Langridge, that great singer, never tired of pointing out that he went to a secondary modern school; while, as to job prospects, the choice was probably wider if you went to the grammar school, but your income was not guaranteed to be higher. No-one seemed to worry about that when I was a child: men in ordinary jobs were able to own a house and support their family, without their wives having to work – they may have *wanted* to work, of course, but they didn't *need* to in order to pay the mortgage. I mention income prospects only because that bulks very large nowadays in discussions of educational opportunity and the ability to repay student loans. There's many a hollow laugh in my business when people speak of the financial rewards of study as if they were inevitable – doubtless that's true in the theatre as well.

I remember watching Harold Wilson's famous pound-in-your-pocket broadcast, but I was thirteen, so it was older people who had to work out what he meant. The first time I became aware of rising costs was when decimal currency came in, just over three years later. I think there was a special department to deal with profiteering (by excessive rounding-up, or just down-right price rises). Suddenly, everything seemed expensive, but sixteen-year-olds are always expensive to run. Overall, my hazy recollections of finance are that things got worse towards the end of the 60s. But my fiver was still lasting a week in 1971.

BN: Having dwelt for a moment on how far it was possible to stretch a fiver, I do think it's valuable to emphasise that you had to duck and weave to start making your way into music. That you relied on the charity of that Baptist Chapel, and had to watch how much you spent on tea. (I didn't know that story, by the way – I used to tot up what I spent on coffee too!) I think it's always important to give this stage in an artist's life some emphasis. No one arrives anywhere without a great deal of support and nurturing around them. Just as it's almost impossible to identify an artist whose interest comes from nowhere – sometimes it's not the parents or the immediate family, but there's almost always an aunt who reads, or a great choirmaster, or whoever, who initiates the desire to make work. Czesław Miłosz wrote that once a writer is born into a family, that family is finished – but if that's the case, then it's the family who's doing the killing, because it takes a whole family to make a piece of work that reaches the public. For a time between your growing up and mine, I think that fact was underappreciated. The people whose support networks were naturally stronger found it much easier to last and to get somewhere than the people who had to look for help. That's an improving situation now, but it's always vital to advocate for the fact that everyone needs help, because at the start, it isn't going to pay. You won't be good enough, and no one will take a chance on you either.

DON: Support networks are very important. Educational institutions have transformed how they help their students, perhaps in answer to the decline of other sources of aid. But it's still difficult to get to the point of being considered for what help there is. School-teachers have an important role to play, as do choirmasters or youth-theatre leaders or scout-masters or whatever. Sport seems to be working well here – youthful talent is spotted and nurtured in many different fields. That's come on stream since Mr. Blair nailed down the Olympics for London, and Sport England was given the goal of winning lots of medals. But it is said that when Simon Rattle told that same Mr. Blair that he wouldn't leave Birmingham for Berlin if the government made some gesture of support for classical music, Blair replied that he had no time for all that elitist rubbish. Now we've got Sir Simon back with the LSO, perhaps there'll be some artistic equivalent of the Olympics, to formalise support for young musicians and actors. What most people are talking about, however, is a new concert hall. Admittedly, most of London's concert halls are artistic mistakes – not all! – but what we need, especially at this point of our history, is some huge cultural jamboree, not another building site in London. You could call it, oooh, the Festival of Britain, perhaps. Meanwhile, hurrah for the BBC and Young Musician and the Proms and the Short Story Competition and so on.

BN: That's interesting. This might sound curmudgeonly, but the Olympics struck me primarily as a massive siphoning of energy and capital away from lots of different things into one very loud thing, in the search for meaningful legacy projects for the Blair government. But you think there'd be value to a cultural/artistic equivalent event now?

DON: I know what you mean. The Millennium Dome, aka the O2 Arena, seemed to have a lot to do with Lord Heseltine's wish to make his mark – and at least he detoxified the Greenwich peninsula. The aspect of the Olympics that I was thinking of was the attention paid to the stars of the future in so many sports, and how the various governing bodies were provided with funds to distribute amongst grass-roots training organisations. Not everything has been perfectly administered, I dare say, but it has made a great difference.

The arts already enjoy more public funding at the performance end than sport ever used to, but even so, you could make a great case for better nurturing young people with an aptitude for the arts. One paradoxical difficulty is that arts succeeded so well in embedding themselves in the curriculum that all that training stuff was assumed to be being done in education, whether in schools or music hubs. Now the curriculum is being looked at again, that assumption is questionable. But there have always been things like Stage 65, Salisbury's youth theatre: the reason you're in the theatre, I imagine. There've always been brass bands and choral societies and choir schools – and, more recently, other specialist music schools. A greater concentration on that sort of thing might reap great rewards. Art is for All, I'm sure we'd agree, and so we'd have to confront Mr. Blair's anti-elitist position. Participation at any level, apart from its intrinsic enjoyment, can increase appreciation of the efforts of others. But performances at the highest level, whether dramatic or musical, require people who are as good at their business as gold medallists are at theirs. No-one thinks, surely, that because not everyone can jump 20 feet, no-one should be encouraged to try?

Drama and music – classical music, anyway – are predominantly interpretative arts: they require a text. The people who provide those texts, whether they be plays or film-scripts or compositions or dances (what do choreographers think of the curriculum, I wonder?), need encouragement to emerge from within the practice of their arts.

Let me leave aside painting and poetry, where the arguments are slightly different – though even these arts, traditionally more privately received, now often aspire to the condition of performance – in order to get on to the political point. Leaving the European Union can be a good idea only if it enables a positive engagement with a wider world, of which Europe is of course the nearest part, geographically. We can only be positive if we know who we are. Cultural identity depends on the arts in two ways. A great deal of it actually resides in the arts – English music, Welsh poetry, Irish dancing, Scottish writing (the adjectives are interchangeable). That part of it that resides elsewhere largely depends upon the arts to communicate it. A particular aspect of British culture is retrospectively expressed in *Downton Abbey*, for instance. As you know, I don't have a television, so I've no more seen *Downton Abbey* than I've seen *Top Gear*. I don't know how much the latter might be Art – but even without me watching it, it brought an aspect of British culture to my attention that I might otherwise have missed. Soap operas communicate a wider culture well, of course. And your plays!

This historical moment, living in the wake of the Brexit vote, is the moment to shout about our culture; all the cultures that have blended here over a thousand years and more. It's not about Little England. Look how the Italian madrigal led to *Now is the month of maying*, how Purcell revelled in Charles II's Frenchified twenty-four violins, how Sir Hubert Parry ranged from finding it easier to set Shakespeare in German than in English to finding the perfect expression for William Blake's *Jerusalem*, how Constant Lambert's music is haunted by the jazz fanfare he heard at the London Pavilion in 1926. My own *Turning Points* owes something to the Beatles' discovery of the sitar.

The opening of the 2012 Olympics was a careful microcosm of all that. It was not without its critics, but it had a time limit, after all. The actual cultural Olympiad was not very noticeable, don't you think? A proper presentation of British culture, over the whole of 2020, say, would put the onus on the critics to step up to the mark. If such a festival were run by a facilitator rather than a director, if it could draw on the oceans of goodwill within and towards the arts, then it could perhaps cost less than you'd ever imagine, and achieve more.

BN: That's a very compelling pitch! And I understand better what you're suggesting.

Now – we were talking about the Gap Year. Can I deduce from your willingness to kip in the font of a Baptist Chapel that you were already committed at that point to a life in music? How had that happened?

DON: Some sort of a life in music, yes, though no idea quite what. Even while I was at Oxford I was still expecting to make a career as a school-teacher. Other doors opened gradually as life went on. One idea I had in my head very early on was that I might be a cathedral organist – I did my Royal College of Organists exams in my gap year. In those far-off days, disgracefully enough (as if full grants weren't enough to be going on with), students signed-on for the dole for the vacations, and I used to describe myself as an unemployed organist. They never found me a job, of course, so I could take the money and run. I hope by now I've made enough donations to educational charities to expunge that particular shame.

BN: Was the RCO exam happening at the same time as you were going after the organ scholarship at Keble?

DON: I think I got my Associate exam while I was in the sixth form, took the organ scholarship exam the autumn I started my hungry year at the Academy, and polished off my FRCO just before I went up to Keble. That organ scholarship exam sticks in my mind. It was conducted in Magdalen College Chapel on an organ with more manuals than I'd ever played on before. Christopher Dearnley, the organist of St. Paul's, I think, was posted up in the loft to welcome the candidates and turn pages. In one of my pieces I became confused as to which of these damn keyboards I needed to play the next bit on, and Dearnley, seeing my confusion, laid his forearm along the wrong one, thereby ensuring, in a perfectly neutral fashion, that I had to play on the correct keyboard. I was so grateful!

BN: Who were your teachers during your first stint at the Academy?

DON: I've mentioned Harry Isaacs. He'd been a student at the Academy during the Great War, and had stayed there ever since. His speciality was piano trios – Arnold Bax's Piano Trio was dedicated to him. Poor Harry was dying for the half-year I had him, but he couldn't afford to stop teaching. He succumbed to cancer in the end, and I was transferred to another teacher. But it had been good to be in touch with that period of musical history, and to be part of Harry's tradition. Graham Johnson, the scholar-accompanist, was one of Harry's pupils too, and it was interesting to watch his Songmakers' Almanac in the process of formation – great monologues about lieder in the coffee queue, if you didn't look sharp.

Then there was Douglas Hopkins, who'd been organist at St. Paul's Cathedral, Canterbury & Peterborough. And Eric Thiman for composition. I was very impressed to be taught by a composer whose music I'd actually played. He was a superb teacher of counterpoint, but perhaps his chief legacy to me was his passion for Sherlock Holmes. I remember as if it were yesterday the lesson where he approvingly quoted short, breathless sentences from *The Golden Pince-Nez*. This is the tale where Holmes smokes cigarette upon cigarette in order to lay a trap for the hidden murderer, whose footprints were caught on the ash-strewn carpet. Eric Thiman, like many Academy professors, smoked throughout his lessons, so perhaps he felt specially close to this story.

BN: And what about your broader musical education at this time – were you able to go to concerts, was there money to do that? What were you listening to? Or were you spending more time with scores at that point?

DON: I was pretty omnivorous as to concerts. I tried to go to two a week. A couple that stick in my mind are Howard Shelley's debut at the Wigmore, and my first experience of Philip Langridge at the Purcell Room, singing *The Bee Oracles* – Edith Sitwell set by Priaulx Rainier. Langridge found himself conducting as well as singing, just to keep all the complexities together. I was most impressed – couldn't have dreamed that this wonderful musician would later play such a big role in my musical life.

My concert-going was pretty thorough at Oxford too. I used to get a season ticket to the Proms, and sit behind the orchestra every night, watching the conductors like a hawk. During term, there were the weekly student chamber concerts in the Holywell Music Room, and endless choral concerts put on by would-be conductors, as well as professional concerts: Charles Rosen playing the Hammerklavier Sonata in the Town Hall, for instance, who fixed himself in our minds by banishing to the back of the hall some of our lecturers who were sitting in the front row with their scores on their knees.

I certainly spent a lot of time with scores. I read somewhere that there were people who could 'read a score like a newspaper', and I made that my ambition. I started with Haydn string quartets, sitting in a deck-chair in the garden, staring at the page bar by bar, working out the pitches one by one, and then gradually sticking everything together. Later I did the same thing with Corelli and Purcell trio sonatas. It worked. When I went to hear Britten's *Death in Venice* for the first time (in Toronto), people chatting with me beforehand assumed that I must have heard it often – I was singing bits that appealed to me, and talking about the orchestral colours, and so on. They found it very hard to believe that all I'd done was to read the score on the plane over. I'm afraid that musical literacy is not widespread.

BN: It's an interesting detail, to think of you sitting in the garden at Buckby and internalising all this, taking it all home with you. It's a lovely place to sit – a sloping lawn down to a hedge where Grandma used to leave leftovers to feed the fox, and then a view over fields for about three miles to the horizon. The church to the right, and open space everywhere else. It must have felt increasingly like a different world, during this period of living between Buckby and London.

DON: Perhaps, as you yourself have described, I became conscious of difference in myself, and therefore conscious of the difference within everyone.

You asked about the culture I think I come from. You'll see from the foregoing that Vaughan Williams and Cecil Sharp and Percy Dearmer, the great chroniclers of the folk traditions of England, were more effective in their work even than they hoped. Essentially I grew up believing, not only everything that was in the Bible, but also that the folk-culture so sedulously re-imagined by those three, especially through that little blue hymn-book, but also through Sharp's Country Dance tune-books – I have my

Mum's copies of those, bought in 1952 – actually was continuous. Elderly men in smocks were not just in the Rupert books, for me.

BN: Without wishing to cut you yet further adrift, it should perhaps be said that even the Rupert books themselves might be considered something of a folk memory these days, despite Paul McCartney's efforts.

DON: There we go, I'm harking back again. My idea of my culture came from people at least two generations before me, in person, and from still earlier cultural entrepreneurs that some of those people actually knew. Long Buckby made it very easy to experience the past as merely an outgrowth from the present. So perhaps it's no surprise that my idea of the future is related, through the present, to the past.

BN: I was taught by the novelist Giles Foden for a while, and he had this wonderful concept he referred to as 'psychic geography' – the world we see when we close our eyes. Which of course is as much philosophical/cultural as it is geographical, a question of tone as well as place. But I'd be interested to imagine a particular landscape, or set of landscapes, that we're traversing. Wordsworth wrote of his project as being to 'connect the landscape with the quiet of the sky' – which presupposes, I think, the necessity of a given landscape in which we can root our enquiries. So let's establish one of those for ourselves – where are the places where you live in your mind, where do you see when you shut your eyes?

DON: I see the view of the fields from the house where I was born – the view's still there – and the sweep of the South Downs from Chanctonbury Ring to Butser Hill, that we could see from our hunting lodge. I see the red, white and blue of Keble bricks. I smell coal-smoke as I imagine the streets of Long Buckby, and the mould and polish of Northamptonshire churches as I practiced the organ. I hear the brass bands I played in, and hymn-singing more enthusiastic than skilful, and always birdsong. (I remember one evening in Keble quad, listening to a blackbird as a fox walked by.)

BN: We used to get ducks on the lawns in Keble when I was there, but I don't think I ever saw a fox.

DON: If you had, I'm sure you wouldn't have seen ducks!

BN: The images you've just offered bring us back to the fact that, having grown up in Buckby, you were then obliged to move away for work, and haven't found your way back. You went on to live right across the south.

DON: London, of course, for quite a while – everyone in any sort of creative art needs to spend time living in a big city. Then to Petworth, where a Northampton composer friend, Robert Walker, had renovated Elgar's cottage and founded a Festival. He told me that Petworth Parish Church was looking for an organist, and was offering a free house. So that's why you and Joz were born in Sussex. I kept my house in London too, which was a luxury, but also a bit of luck when things went wrong. You moved to Putney, and I went back to Harlesden. Then my subsequent marriage to an American from the sparsely populated state of Maine meant that I moved to empty Salisbury

Plain, about the time that you moved to Salisbury itself. When things went wrong again, I moved into Andover, handily just up the railway line from Salisbury.

BN: Discovering London must have changed the way you saw the world.

DON: After Oxford I went back to the Academy. Uncle John was working for a property developer, and he found me a flat in Covent Garden. It was supposed to be a temporary arrangement while they got round to knocking it down, but I was there for three or four years, and in fact the building's still standing. That flat was a great place for parties. I found myself in a lot of student competitions, and they often ended up with a concert in the Purcell Room, which was just a short walk away. My parties afterwards became very popular. I remember walking up my stairs with a gate-crasher who asked me if I knew the chap who was throwing the party. That was our friend, the writer Simon Mundy, who I've known for forty years now. It was at another party, at Nick Kenyon's, that I met Jumbo – David Wilson-Johnson, with whom I've done such a lot. Through him I got a job playing for singing lessons with Helga Mott, whose splendid address was Number Three, The Wardrobe, Richmond Palace – Henry VII obviously had a lot of clothes.

BN: Note to historians – that's Dad's attempt at a joke…

DON: Thank you, I'm here all week.
    It was that Covent Garden flat that introduced me to opera – I made lots of friends at the two nearby opera houses, and had comps for Covent Garden or the Coli at least once a week. It

introduced me to the theatre too. Someone must have misheard me practising, because one evening I got a phone call. 'Do you play the harp?' 'No.' 'That's a shame, because this is the Royal Shakespeare Company, and we're looking for an MD for our New York trip, and there's a little harp part.' Pause, thinking hard. 'Oh, the *harp*??' I hurried down to the Aldwych, where the RSC was based, assured them that I was allowed to borrow their harp, strapped it to my back, got on my motorbike, and wobbled up the A12 to Aldeburgh, where I was studying with Artur Balsam. In between Haydn sonatas I taught myself the harp. I got the job, though in fact the New York trip never came off.

London was a place so full of opportunity that I contrived to carry on living there while also living in Paris, studying with Yvonne Lefebure on a Rotary Scholarship. Keeping one toe in my London flat meant that I may not have made the most of Paris – I have no enduring friends there these days. And Mme Lefebure and I had a terrible row about the Schumann Concerto, which led to me going off round Europe in a huff, eking out a living by accompanying singing competitions in Vienna and Gent and Munich. In Munich I lived in a lovely house in a forest, with an elderly sculptress who was the widow of the great pianist, Edwin Fischer. Weird life.

BN: In Sussex, you developed quite a relationship with Elgar's former home, because Bob Walker was living there. How important was that? Had Elgar loomed as large before that time?

DON: Long before I actually lived in Petworth, I used to spend Christmasses at Brinkwells. Bob was always very generous, and it's such a fairy-tale place – even got snowed in one year, which was magical if inconvenient. Jumbo and I gave a concert of Elgar songs in the house for the Petworth Festival, and unbelievably, some of the people who came were reminiscing about the patterns on the Elgars' curtains, some sixty years before. I think that was the seed of my subsequent overwhelming interest in Elgar and his music. For the full flowering of that seed, I have to thank another of my Covent Garden parties. In one of those Purcell Room concerts I played Arnold Bax's Second Sonata, and was unforgivably inaccurate in my programme note. After the show, a bearded man rushed into the Green Room with a wild glint in his eye. 'Where have you found that letter?' he cried. That was my introduction to the great scholar, Lewis Foreman. I'd misquoted a letter about the wrong sonata. But the post-concert party put all to rights, and in fact that concert is cited in Lewis's book on Bax, for the second edition of which I wrote the Foreword. One of the first projects that Lewis arranged with me was a Wigmore concert to include Karg-Elert's piano transcription of Elgar's First Symphony, and it was that experience that really turned me on to Elgar.

BN: And was it at that time that you also struck up the relation-ship you have with Shulbrede Priory, Parry's daughter's former home?

DON: No, that came about in a curious way much later, after I'd started to play early pianos. A friend of mine asked me to bring my 1828 Broadwood to Guildford for a concert. I'm very interested in deducing the temperament, that's to say, the tuning method, for which a piano piece was conceived, by analysing the harmonies it uses. Most people still think that our modern way of tuning, equal temperament, was universal by about 1800, but have I got news for them! Anyway, I'd found a beautiful Schubertian piano sonata by Sir Hubert Parry, obviously not conceived for equal temperament, and I played it in Guildford on my Broadwood, appropriately tuned. The sonata isn't played much (it sounds much less attractive in equal temperament), and so Laura Ponsonby and Kate Russell, Parry's great-grand-daughters, came to the concert – Shulbrede Priory isn't far from Guildford.

BN: I think of you as someone who's quite affected by the environments in which musicians lived, the furniture of their lives. You've done a lot of radio work that roots composers and writers in their environments; you're always thrilled to play the pianos of composers. Do you feel you get something from it? You feel closer to them, or understand them differently?

DON: Pianos that belonged to composers are particularly thrilling. Sometimes when I play Elgar's piano, I sense him standing behind me. And certainly that instrument has taught me a great deal about his music, especially the placement of arpeggio marks. Sounds a small thing, but it all builds up a picture. Vaughan Williams's upright was a real ear-opener. Everything that RVW composed after 1904 (so that's everything we've ever heard of except *Linden Lea*) was composed at this tiny instrument. I was asked to mark its arrival at his boyhood home, Leith Hill Place, by playing it all day – actually got a live spot on television news. What the day taught me was that because of its modest construction – it's straight-strung, for instance, which means that the resonance is reduced because the strings don't cross – the individual notes of chords are unusually clear. Perhaps because it's usually the *blend* of a chord that gives it harmonic direction, this lack of blend meant that the harmonic direction of chords was much less fixed than usual. Which is perhaps the leading characteristic of RVW's music! I found myself improvising in the style of Vaughan Williams without conscious thought – it was simply where my fingers took me, on that little Honeysuckle piano.

But you're right, it's not just pianos, it's places. The places those radio programmes about writers' lives have taken me to have been extraordinary. Sitting in the famous room at the Cadogan Hotel where Oscar Wilde was arrested, for instance, in the company of Wilde's grandson, whose voice is exactly like the descriptions of Oscar's voice – a brown velvet cello. Even more extraordinary was sitting in Thomas Hardy's study at Max Gate, listening to the story of how his wife died in the room above – that death that unlocked everything he'd ever felt about her – but he couldn't go up to her.

BN: Moving to Salisbury Plain must have been a completely new context, unlike anywhere else you'd been before. I'm something of an aficionado of that landscape now, having written a play called *Echo's End* recently that told a story about Bulford. And I've fallen in love with it in the way I think Edward Thomas and W.H. Hudson and Thomas Hardy fell in love with it; as the most extraordinarily resonant, echoey place. But 'resonant' may not be the adjective of choice for one who lived there full time.

DON: One of life's mercies – my life, anyway – is that troubles fade, while joys remain. So if I think hard, I know that I didn't much enjoy living on the Plain. One of the unexpected difficulties was that it frequently stank. I heard they used to spread untreated cess-pit pumpings onto the fields, but whether that was true or not, there were still the flies from the pig unit and the chicken farm. And it was a long way to buy a box of matches – I was still smoking at that time. But what I remember more, is walking up onto the down, along the green ways, past the barrow wonderfully called Godsbury, watching the boxing hares and the goshawks, counting the eighteenth-century milestones, still just as they were when Parson Woodforde used to walk that way from Somerset back to Oxford, putting up at The Crown at Everleigh.

BN: I have this idea that the modern traditions of travel writing and nature writing and indeed psychogeography owe a deal to the Plain. Because Richard Jefferies and Thomas and Hudson undoubtedly stand somewhere near the start of those tracks. The way I see it, Thomas and Hudson were lured down there out of an interest in Jefferies, who was born outside Swindon, and then the sense of absence in the landscape prompted reflection, prompted writing. Out of that fortunate accident, Jefferies being born where he was, several great traditions rise up, which might not have happened in the same way if he'd been born in the Cotswolds. Thomas's temperament would certainly have been far less well suited to anywhere else!

After Salisbury Plain, you ended up in Andover. The roads around the town must have felt like a return, both to Northamptonshire and to Sussex; a familiar environment, even if the town of Andover itself wasn't.

DON: Yes, Andover was the first proper town I'd ever lived in (apologies to Petworth, but you know what I mean). I'd lived in villages, in cities, in several middles of nowhere – and this oddly convenient thing, a town, really pleased me. I could bike to Waitrose, for heaven's sake. There are banks, coffee shops! Yet, a short walk from the house, there are The Lakes, a place we both love, I think. Just flooded gravel pits, but a stronghold of Nature: I've seen glow-worms and kingfishers there.

And yes, it is the roads, the lanes, round Andover that have made it such a good place to live. On my bike, it takes me about four minutes to reach a place where I can't see any houses at all. Once you're five miles away uphill, you're in a landscape that I've come to love very much. Some of the views are very like those from the hunting-lodge in Petworth, where we could survey the South Downs. But some are more charming, smaller scale, and it's those undulating corners that I find most beautiful – the gradual unfolding of a new valley, the heaving into view of a wood as I breast a ridge.

BN: Andover must be the place you've lived longest since you left home, but at the time we're writing this book, you're in the process of moving on again. How does that feel?

DON: I've sold my house in Andover, but I'm not sure where I'll be moving next. Looking at innumerable houses, but you have to kiss a lot of frogs, don't you? I want somewhere big enough to put most of my pianos. Not back to Northamptonshire, I think. Time for something new. I'm very excited about that.

BN: I'm hoping to give readers a sense of the way you see, but of course it's slightly disingenuous to do this by referring to places alone. The world tends to take on a continuous tone, I think, it tends to look the way we see it, our perceptions form so much of our reality, so these locations don't tell the whole story. But I hope they give a flavour. We find ourselves orbiting a central human problem – the possibility of expressing the self, and of knowing what self to express. Because even to ask you to map your England is to cage you, isn't it, you're someone who's been formed to a significant extent by the cultures of other countries and continents as well.

DON: As I said, I was based in Paris for a year, living here and there in Europe, and I spent most of the nineties in America. Musicians are fortunate touring creatures.

BN: Music, like musicians, is never only from one place either, is it.

DON: Music's relation to place takes a lot of thinking about. I do hear cultural characteristics in different musical traditions – most of the (classical) music the world wants to listen to is Germanic, for example. So much so that we scarcely notice that it *is* Germanic.

How one engages with the existence of those different cultures is an interesting question. Any musician who's captivated by his own culture must consider the possibilities very carefully. One could go through life being a mere exotic, absorbed completely in the specialism one has happened upon – which somehow cheapens the culture. Or one can choose to view other musics through a particular cultural lens. Or one could adopt an international attitude. I meet many people who take the latter approach to life, but I find myself reflecting rather sadly that many of them have simply forgotten their roots. Perhaps that's because they don't need roots, and I do!

My personal culture, as you point out, is not narrowly English. From one point of view, it's much narrower than that. And from another point of view, its place in the wide world is defined by my own gleanings from others. It's a complicated question, and it resides, as you say, not in the Nation, not in the Village, not even in the World, but in the Self that all those things have made.

BN: Auden proposed that 'music is international'. How far do you go along with that? You see validity in referring to distinct musical cultures tied to national bodies – 'English music', for example?

DON: Auden was an artist working in one particular language, less universal then than it is now. He may have been thinking of Haydn's remark that *his* language was universal. I know what Haydn meant, but I'm not sure he was right – the mental equipment required to keep up with Haydn means that most people much prefer Mozart, for a start. At a deeper level, I remember James Galway saying that most people in the world had heard some classical music by now, and if they'd been going to like it, they'd had the chance, and most of them didn't. But everyone likes some sort of music – I tried to make a radio programme once about people who didn't like music at all, and we couldn't find any. But everyone hates some sort of music, so that had to do.

Popular music is predominantly American, as the accents adopted to sing it proclaim. You'd know whether there's any truly popular actually International pop music. I'm regarding Abba and the Beatles and the Stones as token Americans, of course. The only 'international' composers I can think of are John Williams & Andrew Lloyd Webber – both consummate professionals, but betraying little of their innermost identities. Magpies, an unkind critic might call them.

BN: So perhaps we're tending towards a more localised idea of music than Auden proposed?

DON: When you think about it, music can't possibly be thought of as one culture that is the same everywhere – that's so evidently not what the world that produces the music is like, after all. So I think the shared characteristics of different musical cultures – the marks on the page, really – shouldn't fool us into thinking it's all the same, no.

I spend a great deal of my time absorbing the implications of the national characteristics of different sorts of music – it's the key to putting it across – so I take these national characteristics as a given. (But again, it's the individual that counts most, not the nation. Handel's most Italian music somehow remains Handel – can't say quite the same about early Mozart). German music has its logic – Schoenberg was actually proud of the fact that the first page of his First String Quartet contained ALL its material. A French composer might have felt that was an error, and for that matter might have disapproved of Beethoven's tidy habit of always 'developing' his themes in the same order in which he first presents them. Ernst Krenek's dictum, concerning his twelve-note music, that the aural effect of his procedures was 'unintended' would certainly have horrified both Debussy and Poulenc.

As to English music, it seems to me to embody that historically-founded characteristic which our friends call Compromise and our enemies, Perfidy. Either usually requires Ambiguity, which I think is an important aspect of great art: that may be why I prefer Handel to Bach, who's so damned THOROUGH. You see it in Elgar's chords with only three notes in them: a German or a jazzer would stuff in lots of notes, but Elgar's greatest effects come from the fact that you never quite know what other notes might be at the back of his mind, until he's played out his trick without showing his cards.

I hit upon a formulation of Englishness for a TV programme the Prince of Wales made about Parry which I contributed to, that seems to me to have some merit: reticence mingled with deep emotion in a quasi-coded language which the English love and understand.

BN: But all these cultures are complicated, aren't they, by other affinities which tend to arise along the way, and connect one voice to another along quite different lines?

DON: Yes, the varying influences of jazz upon two composers I love, Lambert & Mayerl, have borne fruit in my own work in a way that unmediated jazz has not. Elgar was deeply influenced by hearing Schumann and reading Wagner. Well into the twentieth century, every other major British composer (apart from Elgar, I mean) studied in Leipzig – except Gustav Holst, who read the Rig Veda instead. Sir John Tavener discovered a voice in the Greek Orthodox Church – an example of how anyone can appropriate a culture, a tradition, if they try hard enough.

BN: I suppose I'm trying to complicate and perhaps even undermine my opening gambit now – my search to define the culture you came from. Because a person is the nexus of multiple different, sometimes conflicting cultures. A life is a Venn Diagram. If I asked you to outline the musical culture you came from, you would draw a very different map that wouldn't correspond at all precisely with the first map you drew for us.

DON: As we have seen! As soon as you think about it, it changes. A bit like Tradition: once you're aware of it, it's dead.

BN: Do you believe that a tradition, once observed, is dead? That has profound implications for what we're doing here! And indeed, for what we both do in our own creative work…

DON: I think there's a danger of that. I suppose it depends on whether you join it or merely study it. Take West Gallery Music, or Psalmody as it's often called – the mixed instrumental and vocal church music whose decline in the face of John Keble's Oxford Movement's preference for robed choirs and organs in the chancel was so vehemently lamented by Thomas Hardy. Two ways of making music in church, one still surviving as a much-loved tradition, especially at Christmas-time, the defeated other usually regarded as quaint history. I belong to an Association dedicated to Psalmody's practice and study. Most of the Quires (that's the word they use) perform the music in period costume, and there's quite a debate in the Association – does that pickle it, or does it give people useful context? It's an important question. If it's pickled, it's dead. Robed church choirs aren't pickled of course, or not yet at any rate.

BN: People still join them rather than study them.

DON: Precisely.

BN: So depending on the precise meaning of 'observed' one uses, tradition very much isn't killed that way. In fact, it's usage that keeps them going.

DON: The interesting aspect of all this is not the Tradition in the abstract – I'm not sure you can have a Tradition in the abstract – but the perception of the Tradition by the Individual. No traditions without people practising them, after all. I got drawn into Psalmody because I came across a manuscript of tunes by the Regency vicar of Swanage, Thomas Bartlett. I was the organist of Poole Parish Church at the time, and trying to deal with the familiar – traditional! – conflict between the Robed Choir and the Music Group. This traditional Dorset repertoire, sanctioned by Hardy, the most famous son of Dorset, usefully combined both, and disposed of whatever conflict there had been.

A cynic would say I was manipulating tradition. But it goes deeper than that. I've mentioned the Keble connection to one side of the debate: I lived that aspect, playing daily services in Keble Chapel. But I have a personal feeling about the other side of the debate too: I've performed so many Hardy songs, especially Britten's *The Choirmaster's Burial*, which dramatizes the conflict between Psalmody and the modern Victorian vicars. The choirmaster (Hardy's grandfather, in fact) had wanted music over his grave, but the vicar thought that too old-fashioned. The night after the funeral, the vicar glanced out of his window and saw angels singing over the grave. 'Thus the tenor-man told' says Hardy (the tenor-man was his father), adding slyly 'when he had grown old', prompting the question Were they angels? or just the bolshy musicians getting their own back on the vicar? I've performed this very often, particularly revelling in the fact that Britten's piano accompaniment is (covertly, slyly) based on the psalmody tune mentioned in the poem, Mount Ephraim. It's a tune long familiar to me, because it's in Vaughan Williams's *English Hymnal* (very Oxford Movement). This whole complicated web of the personal and the traditional means still more to me since I made a radio programme called *Thomas Hardy's iPod*, which took me to Stinsford Church. (Making a radio programme, like any other creative act, generates a feeling of ownership.) The first three gravestones are of Thomas Hardy, choirmaster, Thomas Hardy, tenor-man, and Thomas Hardy, poet, and you can see the windows where 'the vicar looked out'.

So, is West Gallery Music a living tradition? You won't find it in any ordinary Sunday service, but it's alive and kicking in my head!

BN: What you've said has significant bearing on your creative work. If it's the use of a tradition that keeps it breathing, there's an element of preservation, or continuation, in your exploration of an English musical tradition. A Proustian project of reclamation through art.

DON: I think you can use the old sounds to say something new, just as you can use the same old words in poetry. They're the sounds I want to hear, and they're saying the things I want to say. Sometimes people only hear the sounds, rather than the meaning of the sounds, but that's true of any music, so it's just a risk you have to run.

BN: Rather delightfully then, we arrived once we got stuck into that little digression at the opposite formulation to the place where we started: we concluded that a tradition *lives* through being observed.

I think both can be true, the living and the killing. This is why I think people like theatre; we're interested in the inherent double meaning woven into every act of observation that means a tradition can only live by being observed, and is also killed by being observed. To look is both to reveal and to conceal. I used to want to write something about hair dye to illustrate this point – to dye one's hair is simultaneously to display, to decorate, to attract attention, and also to cover up and hide what is there. Once you think about it, you realise the same is true for everything. All acts of performance are simultaneous acts of revelation and covering up.

I think that means all acts of observation contain the same paradox as well, not just the observation of tradition. Because what is an act of performance? It's something done for someone, isn't it? That's Peter Brook – 'I can take an empty space and call it a bare stage. A man walks across an empty space whilst someone else is watching him, and this is all that is needed for an act of theatre to be engaged.' So the audience is half the thing that enables a performance, the seeing eye is necessary for that paradoxical act of revelation and concealment to take place. So observation renders us complicit in the act observed, because that's why the act can be said to occur. Therefore, when we look at anything, we're engaging in a simultaneous act of concealment and revelation ourselves, observation is never passive, it's always active, and it always has these two opposing effects.

DON: That's a splendid paradox, that traditions live *and* die by being observed – I remember wading through some educational report that explained that the act of measuring something changes it. Physicists talk of the Observer Effect, which comes close to saying that just looking at something changes it – at any rate, you can't see something till you shine a light on it.

I spend some of my time working out exactly how Mendelssohn played his *Songs Without Words*. I've an idea that he didn't play so strictly in time as people reported: the reports are unwittingly false because Mendelssohn was *convincing*! The clues that I base my theories upon are to be found in music right up to the Great War. But by the later twentieth century, the habit was to play all this music as strictly in time as Mendelssohn was supposed to have done. My hypothesized tradition was entirely dead. But more and more of us, especially people who play early pianos, are set upon reviving it. And we're reviving it for our own contemporary reasons. Back in 1990 I made a television programme about Authentic Performance, as it was called then, interviewing people like John Eliot Gardiner and Roger Norrington, on the one side, and Pierre Boulez and Alfred Brendel on the other. Brendel professed himself happy with all early instruments *except the piano*, which, he said, was manifestly imperfect – a very personal relationship with Tradition! Boulez, with a rhetorical shrug, asked whether he should go round digging up the original audiences. Tempers flared on the other side, with some very questionable absolutist philosophy, but Norrington frankly admitted that the reason he was interested in how 'They' might have done it was because he preferred those effects in the Here and Now. The same is true for those of us who study Mendelssohn's expression marks, or recordings of pianists who knew Brahms – we find things we can *use*.

BN: So it's the use of a tradition rather than the tradition in and of itself where value lies. That strikes me as quite a rich thought in a musical context. It gives you space to use things as you wish to.

DON: Exactly. Some like to describe this as post-modernism, but I think it's the way things often worked. The young Mozart in Mannheim, for instance, discovering a really good orchestra for the first time, and putting its gimmicks to work in his own compositions. The difference between that and the sort of thing we've been considering is the newness of Mannheim manner-isms. Historical perspective wasn't an important part of a composer's equipment. But towards the end of his life, Mozart discovered J.S. Bach, and was affected by the style. Beethoven called Handel 'the master of us all'. For the late eighteenth century musical world, the mid-eighteenth century was quite a way back. Handel's music never died, so it was in fact the Bach Revival (largely Mendelssohn's doing) that put the idea of rescuing old music into people's heads. But when Chopin makes powerful use of elements of Bach's style, no-one thinks he's being post-modern, picking up an old tradition and making his own use of it. They just think Chopin's been influenced by Bach.

BN: But do we have that luxury of being able to pick and choose available to us when we talk about traditions and cultures and inheritances in our lives, rather than in a musical context? Peter Gill said to me once that to go into the theatre was to set aside one's background and class – I understand what he meant to a point, but I couldn't help notice that the thought was being uttered by someone who has been more totally preoccupied by their background and class than almost any other artist I know. So is there perhaps a sense in which we might be able to try on musical cultures like so many outfits, in life we find ourselves less free to choose our selves?

DON: This is a phenomenon I've observed as some early-formed composers I know have settled down. The style in which they were taught to write seems to have nothing whatever to do with their lives or their opinions – possibly because it never had anything to do with their experiences. I somehow expect a particular sort of person to write a particular sort of music, but perhaps that's just my incurable romanticism. There's no reason why unconventional music can't be written by someone with a conventional life-style. Probably.

BN: In actual fact, Yeats is on record somewhere stating that he dressed conservatively in order to be able to think radically. I can't remember the reasoning.

DON: It's a splendid statement! Worth more without the reasoning than with, I'd say.

BN: This first dialogue is titled 'listening', because I wanted to start by thinking around the way we absorb the world in the process of becoming ourselves. I wonder whether I could focus in on that act now, and ask how music first found its way to the centre for you? You've talked about birdsong. What was the route from there?

DON: I was obsessed with bird books when I was a child – significantly, the books were even more important to me than the birds. My introduction to the delights of second-hand book-shops was through my pursuit of Volume Three (rare) of T.A. Coward's *Birds of the British Isles and their Eggs*, which I finally tracked down in Winchester – it's a shoe shop now. (Ah, my vanishing world!) One *new* bird book I acquired was E.A. Armstrong's *Study of Birdsong*, which quickly *became* rare because of a warehouse fire. This was a book which asked the question Why do birds sing? and its dry scholarly approach really appealed to my ten-year-old seriousness. I began to notice birdsong in a new way. Looking back, I can see that this causational approach to birdsong chimes absolutely with my conviction that music is an activity, a performance with an audience (Why do musicians play?), rather than an abstract beauty.

Though it was an abstraction, a geometrical one, that first brought me to the piano. My brother John showed me how to play *Good King Wenceslas* in the key of F. The key is important, because it demands just one black note (the B flat). I was four, and the fact that you had to choose a black note at just this one place satisfied me in the extreme. How very interesting, I thought, and began sixty-odd years so far of pattern-making at the keyboard.

My country bike-rides are very low-tech affairs, and the whistle of the wind rarely obscures the gurgle of the chaffinch, the bell of the great tit, the scolding scream of the buzzard, the plaintive whining stammer of the yellowhammer, the angry tutting of the wren, and many more such anthropomorphic misrepresentations. I find that on my rides, I often create cadential progressions in my head, and now I think of it, it occurs to me that perhaps I do that to contain and order the bird sounds.

The idea of birdsong and music inevitably takes us to Olivier Messiaen, who spent the last part of his life sitting in the remote French countryside transcribing as piano music everything he heard and saw – not just the bird noises themselves, but the shimmer of the cooling rocks, the lush grey-greens of the willows, all perceived as chords. Messiaen was at an advantage here, I suppose, thanks to his synaesthesia, that condition where sounds can be experienced as textures or colours – in a lot of his earlier music he writes delicious chords which he describes in the score as 'bleu-orange'.

My introduction to Messiaen's bird-world was at Oxford, where I took part in a performance of *Oiseaux Exotiques*. I played the keyed glockenspiel, and the whole part was given over to the song of the Red-Backed Tanager, as far as I recall. So I'd be counting my rests, and then go *Tin-twiddle-tum-tum-tum-tum-tum-tah* a couple of times, before dodging back into the rainforest. About this time, a friend of mine, Trevor Hold, wrote a bird-piece about a completely invented bird, *The Blue Firedrake*, which struck me as a splendid idea. No-one's followed it up.

BN: How much of what has influenced you do you think you curated, or have you been susceptible to hearing whatever sounds were being made?

DON: Well, a bike-ride is an odd sort of curatorial activity, but that's what it's doing, isn't it? It may be that the rhythm of birdsong has influenced my melodies. It's a free sort of rhythm, but free only on its own bodily terms, as the little lungs pant and the little wings beat, imposing order on the sounds.

I've always been interested in the sounds around me – I once made a radio programme about ambient sound, I remember. I very rarely have music on – there's enough of that in my head – but I like to hear the sounds of the house or the town. And some of them find their way into my music. A notable example is the office photocopier, which makes an appearance in the slow movement of my Symphony. There it has two functions. Harmonically, it's a rather beautiful and hypnotically repetitive sequence, with no feeling of progression – musically useful at the points where I place it. And symbolically, it represents impotent mechanical reproduction. You might think that unless you know that particular photocopier sound, the symbolism would be lost. But in fact, because the photocopier chords *are* the product of impotent mechanical reproduction, they carry something of that message intrinsically.

I try to extract the same sort of double meanings from the actual musical sounds I make use of – borrow might be a truer word. Different harmonic languages imply different worlds, so it's possible to choose the theatre, as it were, where you want to engage with your listener. If you understand the processes of those harmonic languages, you can adapt them to express your own thoughts, which will not be the thoughts of those who developed the language in the first place. One very obvious example – the particular effect of Elgar's *Nimrod* is due to his treatment of unprepared, upward-resolving discords – sorry for the jargon, but you can read endless eulogies to *Nimrod* without ever coming across this basic technical point. If you notice the technical point, you can then adapt it to express something else, something of your own. The music will sound vaguely Elgarian, of course – the risk you run is that's the only thing people will notice. Even Brahms had this problem with his First Symphony. The tune sounds like the Ode to Joy, people complained, drawing from Brahms the observation 'well, any fool can hear that'.

BN: I wanted to ask you about Britten. While we've been writing this, I've been reading your old flat-mate John Bridcut, who of course is best known as a documentary film maker, and made a show once called *Britten's Children* (in which we both appear!), about Britten's relationship with the young and with youth. He ended up expanding this material into a quite brilliant book.

One thing that struck me, reading the book, was the extent to which Britten seemed to use music as a way of continuing to rebuild the sandcastle, so to speak, even as the tide came in – long after the tide had swallowed up the initial castle of his childhood, in fact. The reading of Britten's work that arose for me was that he used music to recover the moment in his life when things felt right – partly because he used elements of early life in his work, but also because the act of making work took him back to the first time he'd composed, that childhood moment when he had been happiest, when he was discovering everything. It was an escape out of his reality, a flight from his age but also an act of defiance against time, that perhaps might even have served to keep him young.

Now, all of this got me thinking a great deal about the extent to which that was my reading because that's what I do in my work (which is true to a great extent), and the extent to which it might be what everyone does. Most of us discover a taste and/or facility for making things quite early in life – so perhaps for all of us, continuing to make things is a way of continuing to be preoccupied with the source of that activity, our youth, the kernel and heart of our life. That's a large part of why I listen to football on the radio, partly because I enjoy it but more importantly because it takes me back to 2001, the months before 9/11, when Emile Heskey seemed invincible and I lay in my room of an evening listening. And that sense of acting as a means of remembering, of existing simultaneously in the here and now and in a distant, unrecoverable past, seems analogous to the experience of writing for me.

The reason this strikes me as particularly important in the context of your work is that you and Britten have in common an interest in using cultural remnants in your own work – hymn tunes, folk tunes. The products of cultures preceding you, or of the cultures you were born into. This weaving the source material of life into the products of one's life strikes me as a tell, when it comes to working out why both of you might feel the need to write. I have this idea that part of your productivity is a way of maintaining a corner of the world, even if only in your head and in your music, and not in the physical world, that still looks like you feel the world ought to, or used to, or could have done. A means of recovering, not quite lost youth, but a sense of what it felt like to be in the world at that moment, of things being off in the future and the world having a shape one hasn't yet interrogated and undermined, or seen altered by the passage of time. Does that resonate at all with you? I think the longer we all live, the more we see the way things have changed, rather than things in and of themselves. Helen Vendler introduced me to the concept in Sligo, speaking of the 'layers and layers of memories' she saw on each street, not just the streets themselves, and increasingly I see that in Salisbury, the city I have the closest relationship with. I can't just see the street – I see it on multiple different previous days as well, I see changes and memories and ghosts. I remember someone saying to me once that going round Cardiff in a taxi with Peter Gill was the most exhausting activity, because he narrated an unbroken sequence of what used to be on each street in the 1950s, wherever you drove. I have a feeling that artistic productivity is something you can set against that accumulation of memory, the building up of life like a coastal shelf that eventually makes places too heavy to walk round any more. It's a way of making a single image, cohering one statement out of all the different statements that are possible. And thereby recovering a younger view of the world, when you saw only what was, rather than what used to be or might have been.

DON: *Rebuilding the Sandcastle* is a fantastic title for something! That's interesting that you should write to recover the past – if that's not too much of a simplification of what you've said. 'The moment in his life when things went right' you say – which summons up Hardy again, the last song in Britten's *Winter Words*: 'A time there was ..... when all went well.'

I'm not sure it was always his own childhood that Britten was trying to resurrect: perhaps more of an idealised state of mind. I remember animated conversations with Bridcut about the musical materials that characterise the boy Miles in *The Turn of the Screw*, and about Britten's use of scales and triads – the furniture of childhood piano practice – in his music in general. That's a feature of Britten's music I sometimes find trying: the accompaniment to the song I just mentioned simply has repeated triads low down in the piano, accompanying bald octaves in the right hand. It's a very clear concept, but it's hard to make it sound good. I usually come to the conclusion that it need not, indeed, *should* not, sound good, which used to work well when I performed it with Philip Langridge, who preferred expression to beauty every time.

For a variety of reasons that perhaps we'll come on to, part of my creative impulse has been taken up with performance, especially in my work at early pianos re-discovering lost ways of playing; and another part has been soaked up writing scripts for radio or television programmes. I enjoy the satisfaction of all that, but it's meant that I haven't spent my whole time compos-ing music – no bad thing, I sometimes think, when I see how many composers wrote too much. I've taken more to writing music since I turned fifty, partly because by then I'd enjoyed some marvellous experiences that I saw no need to repeat, if instead I could use the time doing things I hadn't done yet – and partly (and here I return to your question) because writing music enabled me, not so much to reproduce the past, as to understand the future. There used to be a proverbial stage in one's life when policemen started looking young. For myself, I found that I reached an age when the present began to seem strange. When I started to teach at Southampton, twenty years ago, it had been a decade or so since I taught regularly at the Academy, and the students seemed poles apart from the ones I'd known. Their language had changed: the pronunciation of 'st' (as in 'student') or 'oo' (as in 'good') was completely different from the habits of the youth of the eighties, and syntax was, like, streamlined. The University gave me a computer, and I began to communicate by a thing called email. And so on. My experience of quite sudden change was perhaps intensified by the fact that I'd spent great chunks of the 90s in America, perhaps unconsciously assuming that though absolutely all around me was different, back home all was going on as usual.

It was at this point in my life that I seriously resumed composing. But, for all that my music uses familiar materials, I don't think it tries to recapture the past. Its importance to me is that it enables me to plot out the role of the past in my future. That's the view from my end of the telescope, anyway.

BN: Can you expand a little on that, plotting the role of the past in your future?

DON: I'm someone who looks ahead in life. If you were to have asked me what has been the best part of my life, I would at any time have answered 'the part that's yet to come'. Obviously that's an easy answer to make in bad times, but I would have made it in the good times too, just as I make it now. But the me who has been looking forward to things all my life is a me made up of my past, as we've discussed. So if composing is a hard-won luxury, as I find it, rather than a means of earning a living, then what I ask of this luxury is for it to help me into that future towards which I look so steadfastly. The magic is that the luxury thus becomes a necessity. At present I'm desperate to write a John Clare violin piece. It's having to wait because of other projects, but I can feel the dam bulging! Like my piece *HengeMusic*, which we worked on a couple of years ago, it'll be partly landscape music: back, as it were, to the Northampton-shire landscape, just as I move to – somewhere else.

BN: And if that piece is to draw on Clare's work as a poet and collector, it will be a return as well to that first tradition you were brought up in, as well as the landscape – the world of Mr. Courtenay's country dancing. Perhaps Clare's most valuable contribution to the world, to my mind, was to have been more or less the only folk song collector of the nineteenth century to have been born into the class he was collecting from, the agricultural workers. Which offers him a totally different perspective on the material he gathers to, say, Vaughan Williams, or Cecil Sharp. What he was gathering, of course, was the same life that led to the culture you grew up in, a century later.

Perhaps this would be an interesting moment to come back to Tavener, while we're talking about impulse and motivation, the past's role in the future. I'm interested in your perspective on Tavener. Like yourself, his work comes from such very different places to that of the majority of his contemporaries. It's rooted in completely different soil to what's around him. And it's also very much about the articulation and celebration of a distinctive cultural hinterland, to my ears – a gathering together of a great deal of life that allows that life to speak to the present. Do you recognise the synchronicities I'm talking about? I think you were being a little guarded about him earlier.

DON: Sorry to be guarded. I suppose it's what you were talking about, trying on musical cultures like outfits, and I instinctively mistrust that. But Tavener found an outfit that suited him, and a persona that marvellously complemented it. Certainly, he explored aspects of life and emotion that no-one else has, and successfully brought them to a wide public.

BN: Tavener's idea of compositions as icons in sound strikes me as a compelling vision of the role music plays. Would you find your way to a different formulation though? His is so rooted in the tradition he's articulating, I'd think it's actually quite a distinctive form of words.

DON: I think you know more about Tavener than I do. Icons in sound – that sounds static to me, which is probably bang on where Tavener is concerned. It reminds me of my friend James Lyons' contention that a tune is a 'myth in sound', which I find much more mobile and dramatic.

BN: Yes, 'mythe sonore', that's lovely. I suppose while we're talking of Tavener we ought to come onto religion, shouldn't we. That feels like a crucial peak to scale when speaking of where you're from. I can't help but notice that what you and Tavener share perhaps above all, which I think is very much expressed in the music you make, is a very active relationship with religion, that extended in both cases into working as organists.

DON: I've been actively employed as an organist for most of my life, except for when I was mainly in America. Before I went to Oxford I played in Long Buckby and the nearby villages. After Oxford I played at St. Mary-the-Boltons, then the Swiss Church in Covent Garden, then St Luke's Oseney Crescent, where there was a wonderful Willis – each particular organ is an important part of a church's personality to me. I confuse the concepts, like some confuse candles with Christmas. Then Petworth, Andover, Poole. Just at present I have no organist's appointment – I'm moving house, after all – and I'm enjoying the freedom. But over the years I've also enjoyed the feeling that I'm helping to keep something going – which is a rather defeatist way of saying I'm contributing to a tradition!

When I don't have an organist's post, I attach myself to some church that seems to me to be numinous. St Thomas of Canterbury at Tangley, for instance, or lately Romsey Abbey. And Andover is a wonderful place to choose a cathedral for Evensong – Salisbury two stops down the line one way, Winchester ten miles down the road another.

BN: Would you recognise yourself as in some way a religious composer? Very little of your work is religious in subject matter, but I feel that culturally, the root of what you're doing lies in the church.

DON: My most transparently religious work is my oratorio *Prayerbook*, which sets more of the successive Prefaces to the Book of Common Prayer through the centuries than it does of the actual contents of the book. That's because religion seems to me to be a process, just as music seems to be a process, rather than an artefact: and the evidence of the process is in those Prefaces. Since religion is an unforced part of my life, also like music, and since my actual practice of religion has been through music, it's not surprising that the two blend together in my work.

My Symphony, for instance, is concerned with the Act of Creation and creation myths of various sorts. *HengeMusic*, with your poems, puts the landscape into the context of the seasons in a way that's straight out of my schooldays *Songs of Praise* (which was occasionally criticised for being too pagan). And of course, my setting of a Laurence Sterne sermon had to be religious, though it's a special Sterneian eighteenth-century sort of religion – the central text for me is 'We are a strange compound – we want, not to *be*, but to *seem*.'

BN: Are there reasons you haven't written more church music?

DON: As I said, my composing is a hard-won luxury, and when I do manage to create time for it, I try to write something that's particularly me – it would too over-weening to say, something significant; but one of the things I know about myself is that my mind works in a particular way, a way that most people's minds don't. I'm not alone in that, of course, but I get a lot of work that way – radio work, a festival directorship, planning a concert series. People often want my take on things. I try to do the same with my music – every composer tries to do that, of course. In my case it means I haven't spent much time writing in a genre which is already well supplied.

BN: If part of who you are is an Anglican voice, whose perspective becomes so interesting because you're juxtaposing a quite complex, equivocal Anglicanism with the present day you're in, I suppose we ought to try and express what Anglicanism means to you… this, of course, is what they call a hospital pass!

DON: I once spent a week at the University of the South, in Sewanee, Tennessee. It's an episcopal university, that's to say, an Anglican one. Its chapel seems to be a miniature replica of Ely Cathedral, and some of the stained glass shows the Yankees blowing the place up during the Civil War, and the subsequent fund-raising deputation to Oxford – boot's on the other foot these days! The shop sold posters, and one of them carried the slogan, over a picture of Christ crucified, 'He died to take away your sins. Not your mind.' With all respect to other flavours of Christianity, it struck me as a good Anglican message.

In passing I might mention that the University guest house, the only antebellum building left standing, had a splendid veranda. Lord and Lady Dacre (as they became) were staying, and every tea-time that week Lady Alexandra presided over tea on the veranda. She had studied in Paris after the Great War – she was the daughter of Earl Haig, as I'm sure you know – and she knew Fauré! And Sir Hugh was full of tales of Yugoslavia in the Second World War, and of entering Hitler's bunker. A fascinating week. But I digress.

Since *Prayerbook* sets Prefaces, it has a Preface of its own, and part of it is a suitably equivocal paean to Anglicanism:

'I have edited some passages for scansion, and occasionally for clarity. John Keble, in particular, seems to have been incapable of writing a sentence without at least one conditional clause. Such equivocation, the quintessence of Anglicanism, generally sings badly, though listeners will hear how the splendidly typical sentence from the 1928 Preface which concludes the libretto reveals rich layers of meaning during a measured recitation in real time that it cannot convey when apprehended in an instant on the printed page. However unequivocal the message of any one particular section may be rendered by such editing, I hope to have restored an Anglican balance across the whole work, which stretches from the mediaeval starkness of the Litany to a compressed hint of David E. Jenkins's thoughts on the nature of miracles. Let no-one mistake these comments on Anglicanism. Equivocation is surely a necessary part of our approach to the Unknowable.'

The 1928 sentence is as follows – I'll add the musical pauses that amplify its meaning:

'We are living in a new world: it is ours – if we are true to the faith that is in us – to seek – to make it a better world.'

BN: The last composer I'd love to talk to you about is Gavin Bryars. To me, Bryars is an utterly thrilling artist. And that's partly because his work is more accessible to a layman like myself than a great deal of contemporary concert music, but the important thing to point out is that I don't think that accessibility is by any means accidental. In work like *The Sinking Of The Titanic*, or in *Jesus' Blood Never Failed Me Yet*, he takes responsibility for the people he's articulating. He fronts up and speaks out what they mean to him in a way that articulates the people as well as his idea. It's all very Terence Davies, isn't it.

I'm speaking in a slightly theatrical vernacular here, and you must forgive me – but this idea of taking responsibility has become very important to me. It works in two ways. As a writer, one has to take responsibility for the people in the auditorium, who've come out to have a good time; and one has to take responsibility for the subject, and do right by it. This is something I've taken from my relationship with Nicholas Hytner. When he got involved in my writing, I'd spent a decade developing a voice, a way of seeing, a technique, a fictional world. All that was in place from the work I'd done with Alice Hamilton, my principal collaborator. But Alice and I had never had any money, so we'd always made miniatures. Chamber music, Robin Soans calls it. What Nick did was encourage me to take on more – to dare to carry more, both in terms of the audience and the story. I hear all that happening in Bryars. Are you interested in his work?

DON: I know *Jesus' Blood*, of course, but not enough else. I listened to a lot of his music nearly thirty years ago, when I interviewed him for my show, and I guess it hasn't stuck. So, pending me re-doing my homework, and skirting round the implications of that admission, I like that two-fold direction of Hytner's responsibility: the audience, and the subject. Seems a good philosophy to me.

BN: You and Bryars have quite a 70s interest in using film in your work. That's something you also share with Simon McBurney, another artist you first met when you were both starting out, and with whom I think you have quite a close affinity, nowhere more so than in your magpie way with technology and source material, which I think was quite a movement in the theatre.

DON: Yes, I met Simon many years ago at Dartington – the International Summer School. He'd just come back from studying mime in Paris; and in the character that later became the occasional choirmaster in *The Vicar of Dibley*, he would tiptoe behind people until they noticed. Ernst Kovacic, a violinist I very much admire whom I also met at Dartington, persuaded him to dance the Debussy Violin Sonata. Since then, I saw some of his shows, and I interviewed him from time to time, which is an odd way to keep in touch. Then a year or two ago, his brother Gerard, a marvellous musical communicator, hatched a plan with Simon where a whole orchestra playing Beethoven's Fifth became a theatrical experience, and they asked me to come along with a Beethoven piano. That was a thing that grew – led, in fact, to my current involvement in the NT production of *Amadeus*. Because of course, Rufus Norris (no relation, although his sister was also an organ scholar at Keble) loved the idea, and used it for his own purposes. But the great thing for me, apart from meeting Gerard for the first time – a real kindred spirit – was collaborating once again with Simon. Even watching him think is a theatrical experience.

As to film, for me that started with songs and pictures. It's enlightening for an audience to have a picture illuminated by a suitable song – Constable's *Hay Wain* with Armstrong Gibbs's *Late Summer*, for instance. It's a short step to Songs and Powerpoints. The simplest use I've made of film has been to illustrate my performance of Parry's *Shulbrede Tunes*. These are avowed pictures and portraits of Parry's daughter's house and family. Laura Ponsonby gave me the run of the place one glorious September day a couple of years ago, and we got movie pictures of the house and the garden (I'm very proud of my panning shots) as well as stills of endless precious Parry documents and photos. Then I made a film plot that fitted my usual timings for each piece. I watch the film as I play, and I know exactly where the picture changes, so I can massage the performance slightly to make sure that the changes in music and picture coincide.

Richard Bland, a sound engineer friend who I've worked with on many projects over many years, made a brilliant film of the barber-shop quartet *Over the Bridge* singing the double fugue from *Prayerbook*. It's a setting of the Table of Kindred and Affinity, with the notorious phrase 'A man may not marry his grandmother'. He didn't just film it; he faked up an engraved slab with the words on it, which frowns down from the walls of Trumpington church, where we filmed it. Good fun.

But the most fun I've had with film (so far) was when I asked the cartoonist Martin Rowson to imagine the characters that appear in Poulenc's *Les soirées de Nazelles*, a sort of Enigma Variations (but oh so Poulenc) in which the only clues we get to the Friends Pictured Within are the flippant titles – *Old but Spry*, or *Pleased with Himself*, for instance. Martin listened to each variation till a picture came into his mind, and then he painted it. The whole process was filmed, and for performance we simply sped up the film to occupy the same time as the variation takes to play. I premiered it at St John's Smith Square, and Martin painted a live encore, Poulenc's *Valse caprice sur le nom B-A-C-H*. Which we filmed too, of course, and that film, sped up, is now my encore.

My Symphony begins with an almighty clout on a yard of railway line – much more resonant than your traditional Wagnerian anvil. We hang it from a step-ladder, and in between performances it lurks in John's barn. And an important modulation in the slow movement is effected by an unaccompanied rain-stick – I had to drive miles to get one the right length. Grandma & Grandad's hand-chimes and handbells I've pressed into service on a number of occasions, in *Prayerbook* and *Turning Points*. I'm waiting for the right moment to write for my portable harmonium ('for use in the Mission Field'). Its most exciting use so far has been playing Christmas carols in an artificial blizzard put on by the Poole Chamber of Trade.

BN: Do you think you're still engaged in the act of listening? Does your mind still get changed? Or does a complete impression of the world form at a certain point, out of which one speaks foreverafter, or does the law of diminishing returns apply, or does one choose to pull up the drawbridge, or are we never fixed in that way? This has become several straw men waiting in a line.

DON: I'm still listening, though I'm probably several decades behind. I'm still coming to terms with the nonchalant discoveries of Joni Mitchell, say. Transcribing *All I Want* so I could play it at your wedding was a really fruitful experience. At the guitar, her fingers fell quite naturally on those parallel flat ninths, that alternation of major and minor third, I dare say, but when you take them away and look at them for their own sake, they suggest a world of possibilities. I've been transcribing Joni Mitchell for years, and her guitar technique has certainly affected some of my harmonic processes. At present I'm writing songs to accompany a new way of teaching young children to write. The melodic material is entirely defined by the pen-strokes that make the letters – an intriguing limitation-cum-inspiration. All the chunks of music need to fit together in any order, of course, and one of the ways I've made that possible is to draw on what I've learnt from Joni.

Those songs perhaps exhibit a few of the technical characteristics of game-music, where the music must twist itself to accompany whatever happens as each unique game unfolds. Recently, several of my students have become fascinated by this growing genre – and I can see the technical appeal of it, as well as the employment prospects. Others of my students are interested in sonic *objets trouvés* – what used to be called *musique concrète*. One recent piece incorporated several minutes of a plane's engines revving up towards take-off. I could see the formal point of it – a take-off, after all, is an off-the-shelf climax – but I don't think I shall pursue that path myself. I shall humbly follow Messiaen, and use actual instruments to suggest the natural sounds – my photocopier came out perfectly well on the woodwind. But students, as any teacher will tell you, can be a most stimulating influence, and even the paths I choose not to follow can sometimes show me the way to somewhere I do want to be.

I should be sorry if I ever formed a complete, final, impression of the world. It's easy to get stuck, of course, and then it's important to ask whether life has got too predictable, too safe. My life has been a series of fortuitous opportunities, leading to some rather odd simultaneities. I was a village organist who played piano concertos at the Proms. I was a radio host who taught harmony. Those multiple identities confused the Gilmore Festival people when they were stealthily checking me out for that award. They got quite a lot of 'Oh no, he's not a pianist any more, he's a ....'. Luckily, they kept trying, and equally luckily, doing more than one thing is very much what happens these days, so for once I find myself ahead of the curve!

BN: I'm interested in getting stuck – it brings us back to the question of whether one keeps listening in the same way all through a life. I'm thinking about libraries. Partly by accident of lifestyle, I'm very selective with my library – I only keep the books I must, and give away many more than I put on my shelves. And I prune, as well, I give away books that have stopped meaning anything to me. This is primarily because I had to move house quite a bit in my twenties, and lived in very small rooms, and had neither the strength to carry too many books nor the space to store them. However, having embarked upon this method of building a library, I find it's given me a very particular perspective on the way I curate my mind. The books I've kept inform the new books I look out, and of course they're new books, but they're always experienced in the context of those I already own, so there's a sense of a jigsaw being steadily filled in, even as I read a completely new piece of work. In that context, I sometimes wonder whether I'm listening closely enough, whether I'm attuned to hearing very specific voices, whether I run the risk of narrowing my own experience of the world as a result of something like confirmation bias.

DON: My library, you'll recall, has two well-defined sections: the professional part, which consists of books about music and quite a lot of poetry; and the leisured part, mainly detective stories, occasionally alleviated by a C.S. Forester or a P.G. Wodehouse. I'm a hoarder, so it's a lucky thing that I read for structure. I can read Wodehouse again and again, just for the sentence structure, and Agatha Christie, just for the skill of the plot-twist. I read fiction, therefore, in the same way that I listen to music. But while in music, that takes me to all sorts of strange places that I'm proud of knowing, in fiction it circumscribes me in a slightly embarrassing way. I rarely read for character or even for the beauty of the writing. You've done more than most to get me to read contemporary novels, but they're often slightly beyond my comfort zone.

I'm often beguiled by writers who pull the same trick some composers try, myself included – to create something with a recognisable foothold in the familiar, that then leads on to something new. At the risk of raising a smirk or two, I found that was the case with Reginald Hill's Dalziel & Pascoe, and more recently I've been overwhelmed by discovering Philip Kerr's Bernie Gunther. Just a mix of war and detectives, you might think, but accessibly exploring emotions that I don't read about much.

While I'm a sad example of *If you liked this, maybe you'll like....*, there is one aspect of my life that drags me out of my rut every time: professional involvement. I'm about to go off to Shandy Hall to plan a Laurence Sterne Anniversary. I knew nothing about Sterne until the Shandy Hall curator, Patrick Wildgust, rang me up a few years ago because I'd made a CD that took the eighteenth-century square piano seriously (not many do), and Sterne had written about these little instruments. Since then, I've put on Sterne concerts, I've written a Sterne piece, I've borrowed some of Sterne's ideas for my own work. Or take the *Playlist* programmes I've made for Radio 4. I'd always shied away from James Joyce, and suddenly I'm arranging his favourite music for Gwyneth Herbert to sing, and interviewing Declan Kiberd in the famous Martello tower. Time to catch up quick! Or, I'm working on Mahler's Tenth Symphony because I've got to talk about it for a Proms interval. *Chord of the Week* for PromsExtra each summer involves raking with the finest of toothcombs through every piece that's going to be televised, looking for the chord that tells a story. So new artistic experiences often crop up for me, though some of them no doubt merely confirm my prejudices.

BN: While we're speaking of raking through pieces, we should address that subject in more detail, the musical context you see yourself as being situated within. Who are the composers who matter to you?

DON: Elgar above all, because he found a new way to compose using melody; and now increasingly Parry, who I'm sure was on the verge of a breakthrough which the Great Influenza of 1918 deprived us of. Parry is very thought-provoking to me – an educator, an administrator, a musical historian, as well as a composer. Did he spread himself too thin?, I sometimes ask myself. There's another composer whose compositional break-through has been almost entirely ignored – and which I consciously try to develop – and that's Constant Lambert, better known as a ballet conductor who drank himself to death. I find him thought-provoking too.

My favourite German-speaking composer is Schubert – the only great Viennese composer actually to have been born there. And my favourite French composer is Poulenc. I'd normally shy away from the concept of 'favourite', but not with those two.

BN: And what about the contemporary context?

DON: I immersed myself in what was then contemporary when I was a student, and of course I carried on playing certain modernistic works professionally for many years. But I found very little that I wanted to emulate in my own music. For the last decade or so, I've played early pianos more and more, and they've helped me to some new insights into musical expression – I've mentioned Mendelssohn. I don't know any contemporary composer who might cite Mendelssohn as an influence, so I'm out on a limb here. I like Steve Reich's music, but – I was going to say, I wouldn't listen to it for fun, but in fact, I don't listen to anything for fun: slightly sad remark from a too-busy pro, perhaps. Living composers whose work I can relate to include people like Robert Walker, Francis Pott, Paul Carr.... I'm getting to know Ben Oliver's music. But their music expresses their minds, and mine needs to express mine. If I'd done nothing but compose since I was a student, perhaps I'd simply have joined in with the swim and been influenced in every direction. But my stylistic path has turned out to be a more solitary one, and part of its value is its loneliness.

BN: You've talked a bit about your discovery of music beginning with listening to birdsong, but I'm interested to know why it felt like a valuable field to commit to? There's the pleasure in the sounds, and in the patterns, the game-playing. And there's the same kind of circumstantial element that lies behind anyone's chosen vocation – we fall into things as kids, and keep on walking through whichever doors open to us till no doors open any more. But is there more to the commitment you made than that?

DON: I draw my students' attention to the Three Aitches – Head, Hands and Heart. Thinking, Doing, Feeling, if you like. (The order is important to me, by the way: some sorts of mistaken music-making start with Feeling.) I haven't found another activity that better fulfils all three aspects of humanity, for all my teenage love of maths and golf.

BN: 'What is music 'about'? Possibly, about the relationship pertaining between the realm of the senses and the ordered object of their perception seen as the extended metaphor of possible forms of life'. A moment of clarity from Brian Ferneyhough. I'm still young enough to find this sentiment uncomfortable – you have to accrue such an armour of confidence to feel comfortable with offering up possible forms of life to people, I think, and I'm still growing mine. But I wonder whether that resonates with you as a model for what you do, for what artists do?

DON: 'Metaphor of possible forms of life' is too distant a concept for me to recognise in the actual workings of music as I know it. But I suspect it might resonate amongst fanatical Mahlerians and Wagnerians. Those audiences seem to seek a wild overdose of certain sorts of emotion, usually resolved by extinction. Perhaps Ferneyhough is continuing that tradition of dominating your audience, taking over their minds. (Remember that poster at Sewanee, about <u>not</u> taking away your mind.) My idea of music is as a set of aural propositions which, despite the necessary passivity of a traditional concert audience, can be, as it were, discussed with them. Really, I suppose, I'm discussing the propositions with my performers, and the audience is overhearing, or spying upon, that process – but they can at least recognise and replicate the patterns of thought that are going on. Which means, once again, that music is a process, not a metaphor.

BN: The quotation interested me because it alights on the hidden didacticism of making things, the need to believe that you're someone worth listening to, and that you have something to say. Can we conclude this first conversation by thinking for a moment about how that might resonate with you, the son of a teacher? Are there ways in which your work grew out of your relationship with your mother?

DON: My music grew out of my relationship with my grandmother, I think. After she'd given me my mid-day meal, I would play the piano to her until it was time to go back to school. Nana probably did quite a bit of dozing behind me, but at the end of every piece she would clap extravagantly, and I tasted the joys of public performance. The four years that I had lunch with Nana without my brother being there – he was off on the school bus to Daventry, so from when I was 7 till I was 11 – probably fixed my mind on musical performance. And I soon started to write things, mainly in C minor!

Both my mother and my father were musical – Dad in a more untrained way – and they were immensely supportive of me, as they were of John. But, beyond intellectual inheritance, I don't think either of them planted a seed or anything (John planted a bit of a seed with *Good King Wenceslas*, you recall): nor did I feel I had to please them, which seems to have been the fate of many musicians I know.

I like to teach, certainly, especially the sorts of teaching that I'm good at. But I've never seen my composing as part of that – or my performing, either, though I spend great chunks of my concerts explaining what I'm doing and why. Those explanations are the only teaching bit, not the actual detail of the performance; just as the programme note might be 'teaching', but not the actual composition itself.

Your phrase 'the hidden didacticism of making things' doesn't wholly resonate with me. Grandad spent half his life (I mean literally, counting the hours) making things out of wood – you remember his workshop, with its lathes and saws and benches and ranks of chisels and rows of planes. I don't think that colossal manufacture had even a hidden didactic purpose. And what about grandma's lace-making and corn dollies? Pure pleasure of creation, I think. That's got to be a big part of making things.

Playing

BN: I've titled this second sequence 'Playing'. Ostensibly, what I hope to cover here is the bulk of your professional life – your work as a performer. But I have it in my mind as well that what we're circling is one person's route into a life, into living well, and I want to draw attention to that as we begin. This book will take the same path everyone does as they find their way into the world – first we listen, then we simulate, then we live. In some lives, I don't think the path is as easy to trace. Not everyone has a vocation. Not everyone's entire life can be expressed as the development of a single project. Of course, your life isn't adequately summarised if we turn it into a single developing theme, either. If we were to exhaustively catalogue everything you've ever done, a meaning would emerge that was too diffuse and complex to express – or you might end up with a catalogue of infinite drift, I don't know how open you are to the idea that lives have inherent meanings at all, or whether it's fairer to say all narratives are superimposed. But the opportunity we have here is that it's in the nature of an artist's career, where the life feeds the work and the enthusiasms are buried deep in childhood and the work is all-consuming, that a narrative can be constructed more easily than is usually the case that expresses something like a linear development through life. So when looking at an artist's life, you can say things about the way all people move through time more easily than you can with some other careers. The milestones are easier to make out. So for the purposes of this book we'll read your performing career as a second stage in a development that leads, eventually, to the writing of music. Not an adequate summation, but perhaps it's an interesting one, you see the two as connected?

DON: It was the break-down of my early composing career that led directly to my performing career. I've already hinted that my composing didn't go down too well in 1970s Oxford, though come to think, I left with a composition scholarship to the Academy. But the contemptuous reaction to my B. Mus exercise a year later – 'This fugue subject implies harmony' was one criticism I still recall with some puzzlement – and the prevailing narrow taste in 'modern music' funding circles, led me to concentrate on something I did to everyone's satisfaction, namely, play the piano. Young performers play a wide range of music, partly because they know they need a wide range of experience, and partly for frank commercial reasons, and so I formed hands-on opinions of the work of still-living composers like Tippett & Britten & Messiaen, and I gave innumerable premieres of works by composers now forgotten.

BN: It's a very interesting environment, the generation of contemporaries one works with at the beginning, before it's clear who's really going to make it. I've been going through that myself for the last few years – it's still a bit too soon to tell which of my generation of theatremakers will one day be filed under that 'now forgotten'. Because there's no precise formula for identifying the ones who'll last, is there. It's not only talent, it's not only prevalent fashions in funding circles, it's not only luck, it's not only hard work, it's not only whether you choose to have a family, or where you're from, or who you know; it's not even whether you're someone that anyone likes. It's terrifying, because of course, after the first six months when a few people who thought they were serious wake up and back out, anyone who's tilting at the windmill of the arts can't imagine doing anything else, and doesn't have a back-up plan, even though some will end up needing one. The arts are so hard to break into, you'd never do it if you were capable of doing anything else. But it's also a very wonderful moment, because, in a Schrodinger sort of way, you live suspended in this moment where anything might be possible for you and your friends – even if in actual fact, when you get to the end, you will look back and find that it wasn't.

DON: 'Now forgotten' sounds callous, doesn't it? I meant it more as a merciful imprecision. Your list of things that need to slot into place is pretty scary – and very carefully ordered! Academy Professors, as I discovered when I became one, all agreed that we should exert ourselves to the utmost to put students off, because only the students that can't be put off stand the slightest chance in the business. Good as far as it goes, but things change, become less narrow – good changes as well as bad changes. Some of the less positive changes at institutions of higher education are down to money, which has all sorts of repercussions – not all new courses fill purely educational needs. Then, if half the population is going to university, degrees will need to change, not necessarily for the worse: but we need to make sure that the former methods of study, where they were valuable, can be continued – which has emphatically not happened in secondary school music.

But there are positive changes too. I'm thinking especially of social change. What's often called dumbing-down (something I've hinted at in the previous paragraph) can also be seen as a welcome acceptance that art need not always be on the verge of unintelligibility to be worthy – which is why my music can reach listeners now, though it was so out of tune with the seventies. Another helpful social development is a public acceptance of the portfolio career. We can take real advantage of the new opportunities the twenty-first century has brought us, the communications revolution. I wonder if I could have created a taste for my sort of music back in the seventies, if we'd had the Internet. But it lumbers up too late, like Chesterfield coming to the assistance of Dr. Johnson. Still, it gives us new ways to reach audiences, if only we had time to develop them.

BN: You told me once that the thing to watch for was what happened when everyone turned thirty – it was around then that things started shaking out. Having turned thirty not so long ago, I can increasingly attest to the truth of this. Did that advice come from personal experience?

DON: Observation rather than experience, luckily. There were so many schemes and scholarships that you could compete for till you were thirty. After that, you were on your own, and many winners didn't make the change into actually earning a living. It's an age that concentrates the mind in many ways. Clocks are ticking, clocks of self-esteem as well as of biology. Is it still too late to become a bank manager? we used to ask ourselves back in the day, in blissful ignorance, probably, of how difficult it is to be a bank manager.

BN: Your passing reference to funding will have been met with a nod of agreement from any other artists reading this. Can you tell me a little more about what you're referring to there?

DON: The student schemes I profited by were things like the Countess of Munster Musical Trust, which bought me a piano, now on loan to Keble; the Park Lane Group, which put on concerts with me in, and of which I'm still a council member; the Greater London Arts Association, which no longer exists, let alone puts on concerts; the Royal Overseas League, whose annual competition goes from strength to strength; the Westmorland Concert Trust, another concert promoter; and, a cautionary tale, the Martin Musical Trust, which turned me down because I didn't ask for enough money, so probably didn't really need it, they thought. Hats off to Rotary International, which took me to Paris. There was one fellowship offered by the Academy, which I won; but I was then asked if I would rather be on the staff, in which case the fellowship would be given to the runner-up. Image matters ('we want not to *be*, but to *seem*' – there's that crucial line from Sterne again), so I haggled. Could it be announced that I had won, and then could I be put on the staff, while the runner-up got the money without fanfare? That tickled Sir Anthony Lewis, the Principal, so that's what happened.

A few people seem to think that teaching is in itself an admission of failure as a performer. I've never gone along with that view. The act of teaching, quite apart from its didactic side, is a way of experiencing music outside real time, like silent score-reading but more aware.

BN: I couldn't agree more with you there. Not many people have trusted me with teaching yet, but what I love about the work I've done to date is that you cede a degree of control over the directions a train of thought proceeds in. It's all too easy, I think, to settle into the rhythms of your own ways of reading or rationalising. With a student, that is constantly surprised and complicated, because you're tethered together for the duration of the journey.

DON: 'Ceding a degree of control'. That's the best sort of teaching, and you go straight to it because you can assume that your students have the necessary technical equipment, being students of English – they can speak and write, they can probably spell, which means you can immediately concern yourself with trains of thought. The technical equipment of music students usually requires more attention, so music teaching is a balancing act between ceding control and exerting it, usually on behalf of the poor composer. However much you chivvy them (not sure if chivvying helps), some students leave learning the notes till very late in the day, and so I spend most of their lessons saying things like 'No, it's a flat, no it's a minim' – a poor use of my time. Then we might move on to questions of pure sound – does this passage require a smooth sound or a brittle sound? And although that question is a matter of opinion, how to make the selected sound can be a matter of instruction. That final stage (where you begin, lucky you!), which in musical terms concerns matters of phrasing, or emphasis, of the balance between sections, both tonally and temporally (that's to say, speed, which is not only a quality of its own, but also affects brute length – often forgotten), of the dynamic shape of a whole movement or even a whole piece – that's the sort of teaching that can only reasonably take effect once all the rest is in place.

BN: Yes, the technical equiptment musicians need is much less instinctive than simply speaking and writing – and thinking in words.

DON: What musicians do can often seem so natural that it must be instinctive, but there's a difference between instinct and internalised, fully assimilated, knowledge. When we say someone's 'musical', it seems almost as if we're talking about instinct. But an instinct is something that's born into you. If humanity is musical – and it is – then all humanity should have similar musical instincts. Yet when I say someone's musical, with my background it's probably because they understand how to shape a tune in accordance with the harmony, and that's something that comes from immersion in the sort of music that does that. You can see it actually happening with students from a different musical culture: some of my Chinese students, for instance, whose ideas of phrasing can change radically over a year. When an Indian musician praises musicality, he might mean the ability to sing perfectly tuned microtones, and that's something that Western singers find very hard: musical instinct doesn't help them, although in Indian singers it *seems* instinctive. My Chinese students often play Chinese music to me, and they display a different sort of instinctive-seeming musical skill from the one I'm trying to teach them.

It's complicated by the fact that instinct does play a part in our reaction to sound: a loud noise makes us jump, fingernails on the blackboard set our teeth on edge, while a deep bell somehow gives a feeling of satisfaction or reassurance. So some aspects of listening to music do rely on instinct, and there are some listeners who look no further than that. But I think the universal musical instinct operates only at a fundamental level, a predilection for organised sound, perhaps keying into an instinctive love of symmetry and proportion that lives in our ears as well as our eyes. Other, more complicated, musical matters have to be learned – learned so well that they begin to *seem* instinctive, like a top golfer's swing. But very few golfers haven't worked like mad on their swing.

Do you remember how Huckleberry Finn, disguised as a girl, gave himself away by jerking his knees together when the wise old lady threw him a ball? Girls, she explained, would jerk their knees apart to catch the ball more surely in their skirt. If you imagine it yourself, the movement seems instinctive, but obviously, it's learned.

How might that all apply to music? I've been studying the precise positioning of expression marks in Schubert and Mendelssohn, and I've come to the conclusion that those composers 'showed' the phrases in performance by slightly slowing down towards the end of a phrase, but then resuming the previous speed before the new phrase starts. Today, most performers wait till the new phrase has started. It seems natural, instinctive, to us, and it's hard to make yourself do it the other way – but I'm working on internalising that knowledge, so that I can convince an audience with it. I hope the audience won't even notice what I'm doing, consciously. But performing it that way has an effect on the overall continuity of the musical discourse that will work on the unconscious mind of the listener, and give the music the effect that its creator designed it to have.

Inspiration sounds as if it should be instinctive – the conception of a beautiful melody, for instance. But I think it was Benjamin Britten who explained what he did by borrowing Thomas Edison's 'genius is one per cent inspiration and ninety-nine per cent perspiration'. In Shostakovich's Tenth Symphony, there's a beautiful horn call that sounds as if it must have simply sprung out of the composer's heart. Instinct, you might think. But in fact, the melody spells out the name of the woman he loved. Fortunately one can allude to these musical possibilities as one goes on, of course; and the best place for their exposition is perhaps the public masterclass.

I used to organise the public masterclasses at the Steans Institute for Singers at the Ravinia Festival in Chicago during the nineties, and it certainly taught me how not to do it. 'Masters' who couldn't be heard by the public, who 'taught' by a mixture of scorn and shame, who unwittingly exposed their astounding ignorance and shallowness (and these were some of the great names in music) – a salutary experience, and a direct demonstration of the role of happenstance and, to be fair, sheer force of personality in the establishment of a reputation. Also to be fair, fair to a great institution, I must mention the wonderful classes we had at the Steans Institute from people like Marilyn Horne, Sir Thomas Allen or Barbara Bonney. Most memorable of all was Victoria de los Angeles, whose potent weapon was her smile. She would sit smiling seraphically at the students as they sang, and they would nearly always respond with the best performance of their lives. One day, however, her smile became more and more fixed, more strained, and at the end of the performance she shook her head kindly. 'My dear', she said, 'there are many ways to sing that song. Many ways. Many, many ways. Many, many, many ways.' And then she snarled, 'But not that way.' A great truth, unforgettably communicated.

One result of my Chicago experiences is that in my own

masterclasses I make absolutely sure that I can be heard by the whole audience, and that everyone learns something new. I often start with some jinglingly memorable mantra – I've mentioned *Head, Hands & Heart*, or it might be *Surprise or Satisfy*, which concerns the few ways you can affect an audience: the third reaction you can conjure, as Charles Avison wrote in 1752, is 'disgust, or weariness of attention'. Both Surprise and Satisfaction depend upon the arousal of Expectation, and a preliminary discussion of how on earth you arouse that is often a fruitful start to a class – the sort of class where trains of thought can indeed be discussed.

The best musical context for the discussion of trains of thought, though, is chamber music. I say 'discussion', but a better word would be 'consideration', because the rehearsal process can be completely wordless. One of the joys of accompanying Jean-Pierre Rampal was the musical give-and-take – I would push, perhaps, and he would swerve: it felt as if we were a couple of rooks, playing in a high wind, and never a need of words.

'Ceding a degree of control' also makes me think of radio. When I started to present *The Works* in the late eighties, the first thing I noticed was the collegiality; how having everyone say their piece could improve the final result. You'd think that after twenty years of chamber music it wouldn't be a surprise to me, but it was, probably because we were creating rather than recreating, and creation had always seemed a solitary activity. That's one of the ways that schools have got better since my day, I think. You're much more used to working in positive groups than I was.

Anyway, other work continued to come in after I joined the staff at the Academy, and soon I was independent of 'funding', as I thought at first. I've come to see, however, that a lot of the money I was 'earning' was in effect a grant from the public purse, since most of the venues were subsidised. My Academy salary was from public money too. And what about all the work I was getting from the BBC? Not to mention the RSC. Long ago I started to feel a great sense of responsibility to the society that was providing the money that paid me. The main sources of purely 'private' money I've had during my career were Gresham College (City of London) and the Gilmore Festival (City of Kalamazoo).

Formally, 'funding' is not a word I came across as a performer until I began to put together research-generated projects for Southampton. All cultures have their quirks, and one of the odd things about universities is the exact way it matters where your money comes from. Payments in kind, private companies (unless blessed by some official committee), groups of enthusiasts tucking five pound notes into your top pocket, hmmm. One jackpot with a funding council, hurrah. Never too late to learn a new culture.

BN: I think it would be valuable to enlarge on your reference to the commercial imperatives behind playing, as well. You've mentioned that in reference to the breadth of repertoire a young musician needs to play. I talked about it in a theatrical context with the critic Matt Trueman last year. He observed that a lot of writers seem to have two careers – the things they write for themselves, and the things they write for other people. Which largely comes down, I think, to money. Some writers respond better to specific commissions – Jean Giono, the novelist, was apparently one, he liked puzzles – but I think Matt was talking about money.

I know I've done it. I've taken a job as a favour to a theatre, and written crap; I've taken a job to stay in the family at a theatre, and written crap; and I've taken a job to pay for my wedding, that hasn't been produced yet, so we shall see what comes of that... I stick defiantly to Michael Caine's remarks about *Jaws 4*: 'I haven't seen it. I understand it's terrible. But I've seen the house it paid for, and that's beautiful'. The simple truth is that artists must eat bread, and that affects what they do. Some take jobs; some teach, which I think is a very smart trick; some manage to score a hit; in my trade, people go to TV. Some come from money, and last longer that way. But particularly in the early stages, everyone has to hustle.

DON: I've hustled all my life, and still do: but sometimes I'm able to disguise the fact. (Not sure if I need to, but it seems more dignified.) Very early in my attempts at PR, I used to say that I'd never done anything I didn't really want to. This was almost true. Deciding to take up the harp when the money spoke was an enjoyable challenge, even though I hadn't been 'wanting' to play the harp. One of the most difficult jobs I ever had was as a TV quiz-master in Cardiff. There would be a mystery celebrity each week, who was kept strictly under wraps until the moment came for them to stride on stage to ecstatic screams from the audience and be welcomed warmly by me – who, alas, not being Welsh enough, invariably failed to recognise them. I started to dread the moment that another famous Welsh dress designer – yes, that one – would find me staring at entirely the wrong person. There were delightful compensations – I struck up a really warm friendship with a very famous scrum-half, and I know you're going to want to know his name, but I was back and forth to America every month at this time. This was the show, too, where Della Jones, Dennis O'Neill, Donald Maxwell and I improvised a complete opera – a pretty high point in my musical life. Still, when the show stopped after two or three series, I did not grieve unduly. Had I wanted to do it? Not especially, but I'd have been crazy to turn it down, and I'm very glad I didn't.

In the music business there's a saying, you're only as good as your latest recital. So I don't think I've ever set out to produce less than the best work I'm capable of, however unexpected the activity.

BN: Of course, concentrating on performance won't only have expanded your contemporary repertoire.

DON: No. Along with my immersion in the new, my explorations of the old became much more thorough. When I was at Oxford, a German singer had arrived vaguely hoping to give a concert, and the legendary Fred Sternfeld – whose lectures were always thronged with the flippant hoping he might once again attempt to sing, as well as with the serious hoping he wouldn't – had suggested me as an accompanist. Brahms, I recall, and a real baptism of fire – I knew hardly any German. Then there was John Bridcut's Festival of English Song, which led me to a friendship with Ian Partridge that still continues. But I'd never imagined anything like the close examination of a repertoire that was possible once I got to the Academy. I accompanied string players and singers, I played for lessons and classes, I listened to endless concerts. Bridcut and I shared a flat in Covent Garden, and passing opera singers, hearing me practising, would knock on the door and ask me to go through their arias. Their unexplained absences led to enquiries being made, and eventually management decided to deal with the nuisance by inviting me to work in the Opera House – so for several years I had complimentary tickets to everything. Again, the new was always to the fore. I bumped into Benjamin Britten (quite literally) as he scurried away the moment the applause began at the end of the premiere of Maxwell Davies' *Taverner*. I remember Robert Tear struggling with a prop pistol as he tried to shoot Raimund Herincx as he strode through the audience in Henze's *We come to the river*. Despairing of ever getting the gun to fire in time, Bob eventually shouted 'Bang!' and Rai dropped gratefully to the floor just before he reached Bow Street.

BN: Evidently, you recall that time at the Academy with great affection. What was it like there at the time, who was there? Were there prevailing currents that stand out now, looking back? This was the mid seventies, wasn't it.

DON: It perhaps says something about my portfolio career that I've kept more Oxford contacts than Academy ones. There were violinists like Louise Williams, Sophie Langdon, Peter Hanson, Nick Gethin the cellist, and then singers – Richard Suart, David Rendall, Jumbo of course. Because I was at the Academy almost continuously for twenty years, the times blur a bit in my mind, but the conductors Mark Wigglesworth and Paul Murphy were students of mine, as was Jonathan Rathbone, who did lots of stuff with the Swingles. I was there at the same time as pianists like Nicholas Walker and the late Alan Graville. I've mentioned Graham Johnson and Songmakers. Irvine Arditti was busy forming his brilliant quartet – I remember hearing them play along with a radio – must have been John Cage, I suppose. Eclipsed, alas, in the same concert, by my first Fauré song, *Chanson d'amour*. I was ravished – never heard anything so lovely. Cage's message paled next to that.

Like all institutions, it was the teachers that made it what it was – sometimes forgotten now there's so much attention paid to designing the courses and monitoring their outcomes, rather than actually to teaching them. Not that we had 'courses', we had serendipitous agglomerations of individual lessons that allowed us to make our own synthesis. My piano teacher, Alex Kelly, has reached almost mythical status after his too-early death. No-one who experienced him could remain the same. I mentioned how Harry Isaacs quoted at me from Shakespeare. Alex outdid him on the occasion that I inserted too great a slowing-down into a Beethoven sonata. I got slower and slower until I couldn't re-establish the tempo, and I ground to a halt. 'Aha!' cried Alex. 'Hoist by your own ritard!'

John Gardner was my composition teacher. I'd met him at some evening classes in Northampton, put on by Trevor Hold, my composer friend, and we had stimulating discussions. But John was not perhaps the man to steer me to write the unharmonisable fugue subjects the Oxford B.Mus required. Two things stick in my mind. John was a railway enthusiast – he and Hugh Marchant, a harmony professor, used to go off at weekends on special underground train trips laid on to explore the whole of the Circle Line, or those disused bits under the Aldwych. For his birthday, I bought him a pre-amalgamation map of British railways. He looked at me gravely for a moment, and then said 'You've put me in a difficult position. This is the first book that any railway enthusiast buys. So of course, I've already got it. I could either suppress that fact, and thank you, and throw it away, or I could give it back to you, and hope that it might stimulate an interest in railways in your mind.' And it sort of has. I've always thought that was a good lesson in manners.

The other unforgettable thing was that he had worked with Constant Lambert, and he had two really illuminating stories about him. I've tried to get these into the historical record on numerous occasions, but they are just too rude.

The Principal, Sir Anthony Lewis, and Lady Lewis befriended me when we went on an international conservatoire trip to Austria. I played Sterndale Bennett in Graz, Salzburg and Vienna. It was the first time I'd ever been in an aeroplane, and my luggage went to Warsaw by mistake. I naively assumed it would be confiscated by Communists, but it reached Graz the next day just as if the Poles were people too. Funny ideas we had about the Cold War – some of them still live on. Sir Anthony even gave me a few composition lessons, surprising me by drawing my attention to Chopin's way with harmony. Sir Anthony's abiding legacy to me is a feeling of guilt whenever I play an encore after a concerto. A Russian did that in Graz, and Sir Anthony assumed an awful aspect as he wagged a finger at me and said 'Never do that!'

BN: And did you observe changes, within the Academy but also in terms of musical fashion, musical thinking, musical practice, that had taken place in the years between your Gap Year at the Academy and your return as a postgraduate?

DON: Not very deep ones. HIP (historically informed practice) was in its early days as far as pianists were concerned, and in any case the Academy was very much a conservatoire – conserving the way things had always been done. I'd remained a student at the Academy while I was at Oxford, anyway. It was the next Principal, David Lumsden, who started to change things, by which time I was a professor. He began the development whereby the Academy adopted some of the reflective practices hitherto associated only with a few universities. The eighties were dominated by that discussion, and by worries about the over-provision of places for music students. I became the shop-steward of the NATFHE union, so I was very much on those committees.

BN: Did you find yourself working with the same teachers, or had that cast list changed?

DON: Alex replaced Harry, as I said, and I no longer studied the organ. A noticeable change was in the choir. In my Gap Year I'd sung in the Verdi Requiem, conducted by Freddie Cox, a piano professor. It was the time of the three-day week, and the concert had to be re-timed to avoid a power cut. It meant there was very little rest between rehearsal and performance, and in the show, Freddie had a heart attack. His last words, as he handed the baton to David Rendall, who was in the middle of the tenor solo, were 'Carry on'. A bewildered Rendall turned to the orchestra and did just that, while Freddie's heels drummed on the floor behind him, then fell silent. Eventually Sir Anthony relieved Rendall of the baton, and made some suitable remarks to the audience. We all went home, terribly depressed. We finally sang the piece in St Paul's Cathedral, as a memorial.

When I returned to the Academy, the choir was taken by the

Warden, Noel Cox, a wily bassoonist with a marvellous way with student singers. I no longer sang in the choir, but accompanied it (as I'd accompanied the Oxford Bach Choir under Edward Olleson). Noel had a great saying: 'An amateur practises till he can get it right. A professional practises till he can't get it wrong.'

A very important influence in my second stab at the Academy was John Streets, who directed the opera school there, and who was the best song coach I've ever come across. He opened up a whole world to me.

BN: Can you put your finger on what it is you value in a teacher? Is that different every time?

DON: A wise woman once told me there were two sorts of teachers: those who were interested in their subject, and those who were interested in their pupils. The ideal teacher would be one who combined both. That's very rare, though Alex Kelly came close, with some of his pupils. I'd value a teacher whose eccentricities stemmed solely from his preoccupation with his subject; because unconscious eccentricity is always interesting, and those eccentricities would cast a light on their cause that would supplement the actual teaching. Different every time, then.

BN: At this time you fell more or less accidentally into this association with the Opera House. Who were the prominent figures there at that time? Can you tell me a little about what you were going to hear?

DON: The man I had most to do with was Arthur Hammond, who was chief repetiteur, I think. He'd been the conductor of the Carl Rosa Opera Company, and he was full of good advice about singers and singing. 'A singer should never start quietly' was one of his maxims, one which probably needed a pinch of salt in the concert hall, but which helped a lot in the opera house.

Covent Garden in those days of limited pub opening times was a place you could legally drink nearly all day. Some of the pubs opened at 5am for the market porters, and even though the market had recently decamped to Nine Elms, the licenses hadn't changed. The only time the pubs were shut was between 2pm and 6, and so all my friends in the chorus, who rehearsed in the mornings and performed in the evenings, belonged to little private drinking clubs. I joined them too, until I realized that the concatenation of sun and yard-arm was an elementary way of preserving your health.

I played for lessons for some of these chorus members, which is how I met people like Raimund Herincx. Some real opera stars used me for rehearsal – Jon Vickers on one occasion. It was about now that I met your godfather, Peter Savidge, who was in the short-lived English Music Theatre, based at the Garden. John Tomlinson, Derek Hammond-Stroud and Josephine Barstow were singing at the Coliseum, Reginald Goodall was doing the Ring at Covent Garden with Alberto Remedios, Norman Bailey and Rita Hunter: and I remember Bob Lloyd (Keble!) singing Sparafucile. I heard *Rigoletto*, *Rosenkavalier*, *Trovatore*, *Traviata*, *Otello*, the Ring, whatever was on, often many times. Overdosed slightly, perhaps.

BN: Can you talk a little about the impact of repeated listening? Repeated viewings of the plays produced at Salisbury Playhouse when I was an usher there were very important for me, allowing me to see past plot and look at technique, it was a real formative learning experience for me to spend that year watching everything four or five times.

DON: Four or five times is good. Not many concert-goers or play-goers have the chance to do that, except with the basic canon, where the danger is that you become so familiar with it that you forget to engage. Hanging on to every moment of something that you won't hear again for ages is an exhilarating and exhausting experience. Concerts don't run for a week or a month at a time, so recording is particularly useful for musicians. It works less well for theatre, though – even with several cameras, it feels so different from the live experience, not just of the actors, but of the rest of the audience. It's interesting how different things are expected of the two audiences. In the theatre you hope for laughter, sometimes: for tears, even for the occasional quiet exclamation. In the concert-hall you're supposed to be quiet – and you do need to be, music is fundamentally aural – until you should do what all audiences should do, including sporting ones, and applaud in some way.

I always try to see several performances of each of your plays, of course, and what I notice is how the differences in the performances can depend on the audience. *While We're Here*, performed actually in the town where it's set, for instance, was quite different from performances in places where the audience had to concentrate on deeper aspects of the play because they didn't know the surface detail – not better, not worse, just different. Or the way the actors in *Echo's End*, though in the same theatre all along, responded to the quite different audiences.

Those differing reactions combine with my growing familiarity with the script to take me much further into the piece than if I merely watched a film again and again. Musicians respond to different audiences too, of course, but in much less noticeable details – a warm audience might encourage a slightly slower tempo for a slow movement, an excited audience might cause a conductor to lengthen a pause or speed up a climax. But a score is more prescriptive than a playbook.

Reading plays is an important part in the repetition of experience. I keep meaning to get a copy of Stoppard's *The Invention of Love*, which I saw just that once at the Oxford Playhouse.

BN: An important text for both of us – I never saw Richard Eyre's original production, but I did also see a revival at Salisbury. Four or five times!

DON: And benefited from that, I'm sure.

More people can read plays than can read scores, but I'm not sure that they do. I find that reading a song or a piano piece or a symphony is a great supplement to listening, and in particular a great preparation for hearing a performance. And you can take that into the concert hall. I presented *Tchaikovsky Unwrapped* in Southampton recently, with Robin Browning conducting his new orchestra, *Són*, in a performance of the Fifth Symphony. My first-half unwrapping consisted of an exploration of how Tchaikovsky stumbled upon certain elements of his vocabulary – falling sixths, diminished fourths, certain chords, all intriguingly linked to his personal life of course, Tchaikovsky being quintessentially a Romantic artist – and having the orchestra play short examples from the First Piano Concerto, *Romeo & Juliet*, and the Fourth Symphony, while I played bits of songs and operas. Then we played explanatory snippets of the Fifth Symphony, basically an aural analysis of it. The outcome in the second-half performance of the Fifth was somewhat as if the audience had read the scores we'd dipped into. Roger Norrington used to do similar things in his 'Experiences' back in the 80s, but they were more culturally based, rather than focussed on musical materials.

BN: Where else was it important for you to go and listen to music at this point? Were there other 'centres' that people orbited around?

DON: I've mentioned my season ticket to the Proms, and I was very handy for the South Bank and the Wigmore. I don't remember going to the Round House, which was very big as an experimental venue in those days. Then each summer, once I'd started going to Dartington, which I did for years, there were three concerts a day for three weeks or so, however long I was there.

BN: I think asking you about whether your interest was directed toward the old or the new wouldn't be a distinction you'd find very productive to discuss, would it.

DON: Taking on the mantle of a performer, but with my composer's hat always there on the peg at home, I evaluated new music in the way I was learning to evaluate old music. I began to distrust the idea that 'new music' should really be any different from old music. Very often, that idea led new music to make a rod for its own back. There's an example in the song-cycle *Tenebrae* by the admirable composer Richard Rodney Bennett: even he, brilliant though he was, was trapped on this occasion by convention. 'New music' was rhythmically complex, and was always played in strict time – apparently. So RRB divided his beats up into five, and then tied notes across from beat to beat, and wandered from two-fifths to three-fifths and back again. I counted and tapped, and put pencil marks everywhere, and when I finally got it right, I discovered that I was merely playing expressively – or rather, it was quite a good plastic imitation of expression. He'd have done better just to write regular quavers and then put *rubato espressivo*. Which is how I ended up playing it.

David Wilson-Johnson and I were more cynical when we worked on a new song-cycle which had best remain nameless. Ensemble was very difficult, partly because of the rhythmic literalness I've just described. So we borrowed a trick from Britten, and pencilled in some curlew marks: Britten sensibly invented the curlew mark to denote a catch-up place in music which was not supposed to be precise in ensemble. This enabled him to write straight-forward rhythms, trusting his performers to make them expressive. The composer of our song-cycle displayed none of this trust, and so when we came to record the piece for broadcast, we worried that he might disapprove of our added curlew marks. He – and the BBC producer – sat following their scores as we recorded it, and neither of them noticed any rhythmic imprecision at all. Very depressing.

BN: So this potentially false dichotomy between new and old music, this was a debate that was going on at the time? Or is it a point of divergence that's clarified for you subsequently? I'm interested in the intellectual environment you found yourself part of. For my part, I found my first years in the arts absolutely laden with ideological landmines – all of us trying to be part of something we weren't yet, with no power, and a lot of opinions, and all the ideas in the world. Most of which, of course, were hopelessly derivative and without structural integrity, because someone had read them in a paper or heard them in a pub, then adopted them without thinking them through at all. Which is the privilege of youth, of course. And a very important, wasteful, inefficient, glorious process. Because in amongst all the dross you drawl through at that age, you also discover the ideas that will form the bridges you'll traverse in order to move on to having some power, and doing something about them. It's only by gathering together a philosophy that anyone starts being worth listening to, and getting anywhere, after all. So were you in the same kind of sea of fashionable, usually hopeless, ever-so-occasionally original thinking? How did that process of fashioning an identity take place?

DON: Your medium is words, so perhaps you were more aware of ideologies than I was. Ideology and music sit uncomfortably together, whether it's punk or Wagner. When I was Artistic Director of the Cardiff Festival we had Plato's 'Music is a danger to the State' as our slogan one year, and in consultation with my friend Erik Levi (whose father escaped the Nazis by ski-ing across the Norwegian border, leaving his violin buried in the snow to be joyfully retrieved after the war, and who is the great expert on the subject), we included music from either side of the Nazi line. There was a terrific outcry from people who couldn't understand how a Jewish musicologist could possibly condone performing anything by Pfitzner. The chaos at the press conference showed that some people apply very simple ideological filters to their listening.

To be fair, I'm very cautious myself about composers and conductors that exhibit the characteristic of gratuitous control (not a characteristic of Pfitzner, as it happens). I got into a great green ink war when in a review programme I made the comment, after a performance of Dvorak by the World's Greatest Conductor, 'that's fine, if you like uniforms'.

But I think you're referring to artistic manifestos, and it would perhaps be good for me if I were to create a manifesto for my own music, however uncharacteristic that would be. As a student, the attention I paid to theories of construction and form was more concerned with *how* they worked than with their social message. The only ideology I applied to composers was a simple yardstick of competence – I gave an instance just now. 'Do they know what they're doing? Can they hear what they've written?' I was learning the art of close listening – I've spent my life doing that – and it annoyed me immensely that people who expected people to listen to their sounds – to create their sounds for them! – couldn't hear the essence of them themselves.

BN: You're referring to Karajan when you talk about uniforms, someone you find highly problematic.

DON: Though perhaps heavily disguised, at heart I'm a libertarian egalitarian, if you can be both of those at once. A particular sort of conductor is therefore anathema to me. Because of the way I listen to music – why is this happening, would I have done it like that, does this performing decision make the best of the material? – I found I was unsympathetic to Karajan's music-making long before I knew anything about him. There may be music that can only be performed under that sort of tight control, but it may not be music I want to bother with – though I must admit, I used to love Karajan's film of *Rosenkavalier*. But that was before I'd seen the piece many times in the opera house, under lots of different conductors.

I find a comparison between Karajan and Bernstein very illuminating. Karajan appears to believe in his own myth. Bernstein knows he's acting a part, and he makes it a necessary part. That's a bit of performer's craft that I can understand and admire – it's basically what I do when I play a piano concerto from the Romantic period. This absurd posturing and showing-off, these muscular heroics! But the genre requires it, and it's enjoyable enough – I play with this whole question in my own Piano Concerto (though there's much more to that than role-playing, of course). The problem comes, for me, when the soloist believes it all – I think of a particular performance of Tchaik 1 by Lang-Lang, which I put into a television programme of mine called *Perfect Pianists* a year or two ago. The faces he pulls, the gestures he makes, as he trots out the concerto's over-familiar tricks..... but there's a huge audience that Lang Lang attracts, to whom the tricks are not over-familiar, ready to revel in Tchaikovsky's frank emotion. That must be a good way to listen to it, almost by definition. Though I can't help remembering that those huge crashing chords 'listen to me, listen to me!' at the beginning were only put in at the suggestion of flamboyant soloists who were appalled by the modesty of Tchaikovsky's beautiful original inspiration of quiet, delicate, harped chords. Nor can I help wondering what the piece sounded like in its world-premiere in Boston, when it was played by Hans von Bulow, the great Beethoven specialist who conducted the first performance of *Tristan und Isolde* in 1865, the very year his wife bore Wagner's daughter. But for some people, too much context spoils the raw enjoyment of the music. That I prefer to hear music through various filters of history reflects my understanding of music as a process, rather than a sonic artefact.

To return to Bernstein, there's an untold tale in his film of Beethoven's Ninth Symphony with the Vienna Phil. At some heavy moment in the first movement, he wields his baton with both fists clenched together, conjuring up a picture, perhaps helpful to the audience behind him, of Thor beating the recalcitrant music into shape. Of course, the beat became unclear, and the timpanist went wrong. There happened to be a camera immediately behind the drums, and the editors chose to show Bernstein's ferocious scowl at the erring timpanist – very telegenic, of course. What follows is, at one level, pure farce. Clearly it occurs to Bernstein that the drummer has it in his power to mess up this entire film – the very next movement starts with the most famous timpani solo in the whole repertoire. And so, fearful that the timpanist may have been offended by the scowl, Bernstein sets about wooing him, all faithfully caught by the camera behind the drums. Little encouraging smiles, and one delightful sequence where Bernstein pretends to forget a cue, gives it almost too late (but only almost, not really too late – too much of a pro), and then shrugs his rueful appreciation that of course the timpanist didn't need a cue anyway. An absolute masterclass in people management, and all delivered from within the same general persona inhabited by Karajan – who would not have pretended to be Thor in the first place.

BN: To me, Bernstein seems to have been an extraordinary figure. Music is quite good at packaging people as geniuses – Rattle and Barenboim and Dudamel might be contemporary examples – but it really must be extraordinary to have been working in the same trade as Bernstein. In the way that it thrills me to be in the same trade as Conor McPherson, say, or Martin McDonagh. Was he the pre-eminent influence of his era? Or does it look like that to me because I wasn't there, but admire his work? Perhaps music was always too wide a field to talk about anyone being pre-eminent. But I know Michael Billington has talked about the equivalent period in theatre being absolutely shaped and dominated by one or two voices – Pinter and Beckett, really – as opposed to today's theatre, which is much more pluralistic and really more like several art forms interacting, when you look at the range of influences.

DON: Before Bernstein there was Toscanini. And alongside Bernstein there's André Previn, who could *really* do jazz – his jazz trio reworkings of *My Fair Lady* (he conducted the film) are simply mind-blowing. A comparison of Bernstein and Previn, and of their reputations, teaches you a lot about the world. Genius can be packaged in many ways – where do you put Sir Thomas Beecham?

Your take on what has succeeded the Pinter/Beckett dominance is bang on – several art forms interacting. Global interconnectedness has unexpected repercussions. This isn't new of course – the art of Picasso or Matisse, the theatre work of Britten or Yeats. All their breakthroughs seem to me to have been driven by their encounters with other cultures. The interconnectedness we have now seems to have reinforced the idea of nationhood for many, and it seems to have torn up some of the old artistic certainties and replaced them with new freedom and possibility, just as more people than ever before are able to experience them. The time of Pinter and Beckett, the time of Britten and Shostakovich, very defined canons tended by high priests, is not likely to come around again for a while. Which leaves us with a lot of scope! I heard one of the recent Nobel laureates for chemistry, Richard Henderson, explaining on the radio that his breakthrough came because he straddled several disciplines. Translated to my work, on the occasions that I don't mix arts, I can at least mix styles.

BN: Do you think that's part of the pluralism that defines contemporary art, the renewed nationalism visible in the political sphere? That's very interesting, because in the (lefty) papers I read, it's very rare to encounter the concept of nationalism with any kind of positive spin on it. But I rejoice in the fact that every new play produced in the UK is no longer about the same middle class white family, with the names changed, and the crisis subtly altered. So if increased national consciousness, articulacy and assertiveness is behind that, perhaps that's a reason for me to be less nihilistic about nations and nationalism.

The idea of nationalism as an engine for valuing difference and diversity has me thinking about an argument I heard a lot in 2016, around the Blairite record on multiculturalism. It seemed to be fashionable for a moment to suggest that multiculturalism under Labour had eventually manifested itself as a kind of denial of difference, a highlighting of the things everyone had in common that allowed atomised communities to share in certain key elements of their identity. So, the argument went, the next post-Blairite step in committing to a multicultural society was to find a way to not just hush up the elements of different cultures that weren't shared by everyone, but to argue for their integrity, and create spaces for those differences to be tolerated, celebrated, cultivated in concert with one another. Perhaps that's something we're observing in the arts now. But it's hard to reconcile that development with my own associations with the word 'nationalism', I must admit. It's quite a difficult subject, isn't it, while the far right is doing what it's doing in Germany, France, the Netherlands, the US and so on.

Isn't it interesting to think that a century ago, it was newsworthy that the Oxford Union voted not to fight for King and Country, and here I am with some kind of neural connection wired up between nationalism and Nazism. I doubt it reflects very well on me, but I'll leave it in because it's sort of grimly fascinating. What's led to that, I wonder?

DON: Hitler made a lot of things impossible to discuss. I've mentioned the demonstration at my Cardiff Festival launch. Nationalism is one of the topics the Nazi Party made difficult, I think. But a pride in oneself, in one's town, one's country, needn't be bad in itself. Differing identities lead to competition, of course, but that needn't be bad either – Oxford & Cambridge, Manchester United & Liverpool. There's an appetite for national competition, sport shows us that. That appetite can become dangerous, but I'm not sure the way to deal with it is to try to magic away the differences.

BN: While we're speaking of Nazism … I think in the light of your views on Karajan, we have to interrogate a little further this idea that ideology and music aren't a comfortable mix, because clearly, you're comfortable with acknowledging ideologies in music where you encounter them, so I'm not sure what you're implying. Can you give me an example of a non-ideological piece of music? Isn't creation or performance always an ideological act? Set against quotidian life, so much of which is received life, where we consume or accept and integrate ourselves into other people's ideologies being broadcast to us via our jobs, our TVs, our radios, our social contexts, isn't making something that bears your imprint of how you see and think and feel a fundamentally political thing to do, concerned with the propagation of an ideology? To make something is to offer up a shape for thought you must be hoping, at some level, that people will engage with; to perform something is to draw attention to one particular thing over others, to assert the value of what you're performing as worthy of attention. This is ideological, no? And in your insistence that your yardstick is competence, you're proposing an ideology – an interest in clarity and effectiveness. Which has much wider implications than the purely musical if you want it to, doesn't it. One can advocate clarity and effectiveness through music as a means of arguing for them in everything.

DON: Perhaps we've got different definitions in our heads. For me, ideology is the opposite of pragmatic thought, a pejorative term, a set of ready-made answers which never fit. You're right, I recognize ideological music-making when I meet it, and even as I coin the phrase, I'm sneering – but that's because of what I think I mean. Perhaps I'm Humpty-Dumpty here, making words mean what I want them to mean. Perhaps the distinction I draw between pragmatism and ideology is a false one. I find it, however, a useful one. But I can see that my view that music is an activity, a process, rather than a thing, an artefact, could be seen as ideological. I follow this path simply because I find it gives my particular mind a great deal of enjoyable thought and sensation. I know from experience that many people prefer to think of some idealised music (in the sky, in the ether, in cyberspace, in heaven?) that has made itself available to us via inspired composers: a view that leads to the belief that there is a 'correct' way to play each piece, and that competing performances are not just different, not just better, even, but nearer what they 'should' be. Bizarre, to me, but each to his own. The *locus classicus* of this attitude was an essay written by one of my students: 'Luckily, Beethoven did not die until he had completed his thirty-two piano sonatas'. Put so naively, everyone can see the philosophical flaw. More subtle manifestations often pass unnoticed.

BN: Again, I think it's important to draw attention to the fact this approach to ideology in music is a stance you're adopting, not an absolute. What you're really saying is 'I think music and ideology don't sit comfortably together'. The implications of that particular ideological approach to music, I'm not sure about, but everything created stems from some ideological framework, surely? Some music is about clarity, some is about beauty, some is about anger, some is about mass consumption – it's all got baggage that's separate to the tune though. Or do you disagree?

DON: Not at all! I'm selective about my baggage though. I like my historical filters, I like the idea of reaching emotion through form rather than sensation. But there's baggage I don't like. I mentioned Wagner and punk as examples of music and ideology sitting uncomfortably together. As far as I understand it, which is not very far, punk started with its ideology, and then musicians set about discovering what it would sound like. That reminds me of Dadaism, which produced nothing of lasting value – it didn't intend to, of course. Wagner only became Wagner (and again, specialists must forgive the simplification) once he'd clarified his theories to himself. (Perhaps I'm using the word 'theory' where you'd use the word 'ideology'.) The way I like to listen to Wagner is in Leopold Stokowski's Symphonic Syntheses, which present the magnificent music as concert pieces of less than a quarter of an hour, shorn of what seem to me to be its presentational excesses and naiveties. But dreadful ideologies raise their heads here: what would Wagner have thought of a Jewish musician picking out the kernel of his Gesamtkunstwerk? This is another area where musical ideology affects my views: my great admiration for Mendelssohn makes me resent Wagner at a personal level. I note sardonically that, before Wagner became Wagner, as it were, he said that Mendelssohn was the most brilliant man he'd ever met. How different his views had become by the time he wrote *Das Judenthum in der Musik*. Some people are trying to put all this behind them – Barenboim performing Wagner in Israel, for instance. I'm still at the stage where I was deeply shocked when Isabelle Faust played a Wagner song as an encore to the Mendelssohn fiddle concerto at the Proms.

This might be the moment to turn to your point about some music being about mass consumption. That would only matter if it were the whole point of the music. (There may be some music like that). An advertising man told me that 'classical music is the sound of EXPENSIVE', but that view needn't affect the music itself. Even Dvorak's famous Largo is not utterly ruined. Your brother Joz did a riff in his Edinburgh show in 2017 about what people see in their minds when they hear it, and the answers are amusing, even surprising – but I think Dvorak sails through OK, if you listen to the New World Symphony.

The competence I prize, which you rightly analyse into clarity and effectiveness, is perhaps the outcome of a life spent in what we now call classical music. The definition of classical music that I set out in my Gresham lectures is: 'music that has to be written down'. I usually introduce that idea to audiences by giving them the first line of a limerick. Most people can improvise a limerick. Then I give them the first line of a sonnet, and it's not long before they're looking round for pencil and paper. With no disrespect to musical improvisation – I'm an organist, after all – this search for pencil and paper betokens a different intellectual approach. Once notation is involved, you can spend an hour creating a secondsworth of music, a week on a minute. Such a score demands precision, its interpretation demands clarity and effectiveness. Because these are my necessary tools, I may have become blind to the fact that they're also an ideological choice. Perhaps, like Molière's M. Jourdain, I've been composing ideology all my life, and never realized.

BN: There's a line of Yeats, 'a single line will take us hours maybe, but if it does not seem a moment's thought, our stitching and unstitching has been naught'. I rather think the ideological wellspring is the decision to make anything at all – to cast around for pencil and paper in the first place. All clarity and precision stem from that first act. I really think it's an area that isn't studied enough, the extent to which anyone who writes or makes anything is doing something quite radical and unusual, in the context of ordinary human life. A lot of the time we only analyse artistic products in the context of other artistic products, so we miss what's so weird and political and interesting about them, which is that they exist at all, someone wanted to record or create this thing. People should spend more time analysing artistic products in the context of what everyone else in the artist's class went on to do, or what bakery they went to, or the pram in the hall. The historic social function of the chronicler or bard as a focus for and expression of their tribe never, ever goes away, for me, because somewhere along the line a child always learns to hold a pen, and then starts trying to draw people's attention to particular things through recording/creating them.

DON: There are fashions in analysis, in ways of studying artistic productions. In music, that has ranged from a study of the inter-actions of all the purely musical material, quite independent of performance, to the social or political uses to which a perfor-mance of that material might have been put, with everything in between, from the price of the instruments or the wages of the players to the clothes they or their audience wore, not forgetting all the startlingly different ways the piece has been performed since it was composed – and the reasons for those startling differences. Edward Klorman, a musical analyst who also plays the viola, has recently published a book about social interaction in Mozart's chamber music, in which it is academically recognised for the first time that when the first violin plays a passage which is immediately repeated by the *second* violin, an element of social tension is introduced, especially if it's a difficult passage. Klorman, like anyone else who plays chamber music, has always known this, but he's invented a technical term for it that will crown his academic career!

The nearest thing I can think of to the sort of analysis you suggest is Peter Shaffer's *Amadeus*. David Constantine wrote a radio play about Beethoven called *The Listening Heart*, partly about Beethoven's politics, partly about his hopes of marrying Julie Guiccardi, his pupil. I did the music for that, and it changed forever the way I think about Beethoven. What we need are works of art about artists – or their art.

You return to the question of Why do we create? Why pick up the pencil? My main answer, because we can, doesn't explain enough for you. Perhaps I'm chopping straws again, but I see a distinction between simply picking up the pencil and actually writing something significant. I've already hinted that time constraints mean that when I do write, I try to write significantly, so to that extent my work has an ideological motive – me! But not everyone's like that. Today I bought a couple of those British Library reprints of Golden Age detective stories. These ones were written by a professional soldier who wrote one hundred and forty detective novels, under various pseudonyms. My heart sank a bit when I read that, but I'd already bought them. They may be fine. What was his motivation, I wonder? You can imagine all sorts of things, but at the bottom, he must simply have liked picking up the pencil to write detective stories, just as grandma liked making corn-dollies. Think of the German composer, Percy Sherwood (yes, German – his father was Professor of English at Dresden), one of the minor tragedies of the Great War. Percy composed really marvellous music – I've recorded his cello sonatas with Joseph Spooner, and they are wonderful. He was up-and-coming – appointed composer to the King (of Saxony), and so on. He was on holiday in Dorset when the War broke out, and he never lived in Germany again (though his brother stayed on). Percy lived and died in a little house just north of Regents Park, very different from his fine Dresden villa (long destroyed, of course), and eked out a living by giving harmony lessons to Oxbridge scholarship candidates. And all through his last quarter of a century when, uprooted and out of fashion, there was no opportunity for him to be per-formed, he wrote and wrote. In the Bodleian there are hundreds of single-sheet piano pieces: rather a pathetic sight, in one way, and a triumph of the simple creative instinct in another. They're not his best pieces, I suspect, but some day I should play them through. (At least it might identify the reasons for my gut feeling that, for all his German training, for all his parallels with Brahms and Wagner, his music contains some hint of Englishness!)

You speak of the child using his pencil to draw attention. I suppose I used my piano for that, and still do. When you speak of 'the decision to make anything at all', I think you're really concerned with what the piece is ABOUT. Why do we write a particular piece, why write a poem about a particular subject? You are indeed a bard and a chronicler, with things to sing to society, because your plays present a particular slice of a particular society. That is their subject. My subject is more intangible, very often simply the reconciliation of different sets of sounds, which may be imbued with a non-musical message. Sometimes the mere conditions of performance make up part of the message – here's a piece which hundreds of singers have bothered to learn, for instance, or here's a pianist showing off – oh, it's me, and so on. Sometimes it's words that carry the message, though whatever's going on in the music (at every level) should reflect the words. Sometimes the message is associative, but again, those associations will be implicit in the actual musical material. I mentioned the photocopier in my Symphony, and I might equally have mentioned the Big Bang that begins it. In my mind, it's a Symphony about creation, so the Big Bang has an obvious justification. But, purely musically, a Big Bang is a fine way to start a piece of music.

Some of the ways I introduce such meanings into my music you might describe as ideological. But as we've discussed this back and forth, it's become clear to me that the real ideological choice I make is my harmonic language. 'From Harmony, from Heav'nly Harmony, This Universal Frame began' wrote John Dryden, and that's about how important I think it is too. Where do the differences between different sorts of music reside? Sometimes it's in the melodic language. The tuneful pop music of fifty years ago has been replaced by something much closer to early Baroque opera, a sort of recitativo arioso, with the exciting new sounds and textures of electronic accompaniments carrying much of the musical interest, and the words, possibly, allowed to come across more directly. Or, there's a song by Anton Webern entitled *Volkslied*, which always makes me laugh, melodically speaking. Sometimes it's the rhythm. Steve Reich once told me that there are two sorts of music, rhythmic and harmonic. His music was rhythmic, of course, and he traced its history back a thousand years to the conductus of Leonin and Perotin at Notre Dame, and ever further back, to prehistoric dance music, insofar as we can imagine it. Harmonic music he regarded benignly as a newcomer. Bach, interestingly enough, he assigned to both camps, and I dare say the same might be said of jazz: 'jazz' is a word equally at home with the words 'rhythms' or 'chords'. That's probably why jazzed-up Bach works so well. Reich also made the well-worn point that musics differ because of the natural speech-rhythms of different languages. This can carry through into music without words: Janacek's hanging final duplets, any Italianate composer's feminine endings, what John Gardner used to call 'the English triplet'.

But to my ears, the difference between different sorts of music is clearest in the harmonies, and my own harmonies sound, to me at any rate, recognisably English. What actually makes harmony 'English' is a puzzling question. Vaughan Williams's *On Wenlock Edge* drew a balanced assessment from Ivor Gurney when he heard it: 'The French mannerisms must be forgotten in the strong Englishness of the prevailing mood' he wrote. Gurney doesn't specify, but the French mannerisms that I hear (RVW had just been studying with Ravel) are harmonic. It's a complicated thing – both late Debussy and mature Vaughan Williams use streams of modal chords, but somehow they don't sound like each other. Speech rhythms may affect harmony. They shape melodic lines, especially through the intense focus on language found in folksong; and, in 'harmonic music', those lines need harmonies. The harmonisation of folksong is a contentious issue – I had some hostile letters after a broadcast of some of my own arrangements – but it was very much in Vaughan Williams's mind as he forged his mature style: some of his harmonisations in *The English Hymnal* are remarkable. One aspect of speech rhythm that harmonists must take into account is metre, which decides how many harmonic steps you must take to reach a given harmonic goal – trickier than you might think. There's an amusing fairy tale by A.A. Milne about a pair of seven-league boots, whose owner found it impossible to get back to his castle. Milne writes: 'Of course, what he really wanted to do was to erect an isosceles triangle on a base of eleven miles, having two sides of twenty-one miles each. But this was before Euclid's time. However, by taking one step to the north and another to the south-west, he found himself close enough. A short but painful walk, with his boots in his hand, brought him to his destination.' Harmony's a bit like that. And because it's a syntactical system, I think the word order of their native language must affect how composers conceive harmony, even in non-vocal music. I associate certain aspects of Mendelssohn's *Songs without Words* with the fact that he spoke six languages, for instance. That's why they don't have words! He's inventing his own, purely musical, syntax, which not everyone has been able to appreciate.

Composers influenced by folk music must also consider the musical mode it's in – the selection of five or six or seven of the available twelve notes, and the organisation of them into a hierarchy. Mode is not far from Mood, and the emotional colour of a tune depends in part on its selection of pitches, so modes bring us straight to the question of national character. It'd be fun to re-write some of Liszt's Hungarian Rhapsodies in the modes of RVW's Tallis Fantasia, and vice versa. Amongst other things, it would marvellously illuminate how rhythm interacts with harmony.

There's more to national harmony than folk music, obviously. I've already advanced some ideas about the Englishness of

Elgar's chords, and what I know about Elgar and folk music is that there's only one tune in his entire output that might have been a folksong – a melody he overheard in Wales which he put into his Introduction & Allegro; and that he once grandly announced 'I *am* folk music!' William Walton, too, can sound English without being folky, though he was keenly alert to national style. His three Sitwell Songs (partly drawn from *Façade*, that brilliant set of parodies) present settings of *Daphne, Through Gilded Trellises*, and *Old Sir Faulk*. The first, a Greek pastoral, nods modally at Vaughan Williams; the second, set in Spain, uses crunchy guitar chords; and the last draws on various jazz songs, from *Twelfth Street Blues* to *Chicago*. Walton's first edition prefaced the songs with the phrases: *nello stile inglese, nello stile espagnole* and *nello stile americano*. That was perhaps considered too revealing of his methods, and they vanished from subsequent editions: but the idea of a composer trying on various styles until he finds his own is one I can sympathise with. You'll recall, mind, that I wasn't quite so sympathetic about Tavener's adoption of Greek Orthodoxy – perhaps that's because style is to tradition as tactics are to strategy.

BN: I'm glad to have pressed you on the point, if that's what I've coaxed! It's interesting to consider all this. I'm well aware it may not consciously be in mind for you all the time – I think writers do well not to bear all this sort of thing in mind too much when they work. Byron claimed, quite contrary to Yeats's position, that 'I rattle on exactly as I talk with anybody in a ride or walk'. Which may have been true. Shakespeare, the claim goes, 'never blotted a line'. But I imagine that hard work got done by both of them in the back of the brain, and they rode the waves of it while writing. So excavating some of that hinterland is deeply valuable, I think.

Resuming our journey through your work – at this time in your career, through the 80s and into the 90s, you were playing a lot, and had effectively ceased to work as a composer.

DON: The only compositional activity I maintained through all this was that of arranging songs. I found this particularly congenial, because part of that skill is to find a style that suits the song, rather than to find a style that no-one's thought of before. And people can tell if it's right.

BN: That's the same game as adapting stories for the stage – finding the form that fits. In fact, you could say it's always what people are trying to do. It was central to the modernist creed – all innovations arising from that movement were expressed by their authors as attempts to more accurately reflect life. The search for fitting forms is a major part of the attempt to write anything.

DON: Arranging a song, adapting a story, is a good analogy, but as to modernism, maybe we're finding a difference between our respective arts here. 'Attempts to more accurately reflect life' bring Richard Strauss to my mind. I once read that Strauss (in his *Sinfonia Domestica*) aspired to depict his wife picking up a teaspoon, though that was probably just the effort of a more than usually sarcastic critic. That aspect of Strauss's work was never 'modern' in musical terms. He was at his most modern in the operas *Salome* and *Elektra*, and thereafter taking fright at his own boldness, as someone put it, he retreated into a language he and most of his audience understood, and wrote *Der*

Rosenkavalier, the score that Britten wanted to look at while he was composing *Peter Grimes* 'to see how the old magician worked his tricks'. Modernism in music seems to me to be rather abstractedly concerned with language and its technical workings, rather than with the truer expression of anything. As to the aspiration to reflect life, I associate that with the *verismo* movement in Italian opera – Cav and Pag (that's to say, *Cavalliera Rusticana* and *I Pagliacci*), Puccini, that sort of thing.

BN: I envy you deeply, if you're telling me your life is like a Puccini opera! Had you set aside your ambitions as a composer, or was there a sense of frustration? Or an intention to go back to it later?

DON: There was always an intention to go back to it later. I wrote an occasional piece, in both senses of the word, but life was unfolding in a hundred ways that mustn't be missed, and which all took time.

BN: I want to try and pinpoint where in all this you found your way to Paris – was that during or after your studies at the Academy? And what took you there?

DON: I spent two years at the Academy after Oxford. Then I wanted to study abroad, because I knew it would broaden my horizons; and luckily my name had come up in a discussion amongst Rotarians back in Northamptonshire, looking for a candidate to put forward for a Rotary International Scholarship. Paris seemed a good idea. I love French music, and I'd spent a formative week there in August 1968, just me and Grandma. It had its comical side – we didn't know that Paris goes away for

August, for instance. We hadn't booked a hotel – we simply turned left out of the Gare du Nord, and ended up in a crumbling hotel unchanged since the days of Toulouse-Lautrec. Everything smelt of garlic, and the meths we bought for our Primus stove was straw-coloured instead of purple. I was amazed that the gutters ran with clean water every morning. We went to Versailles, and only after we got home again did we realize we'd been looking round the Grand Trianon rather than the Palace itself. So we had to go again. All salutary stuff, but most salutary of all was the fact that when we went to see Rossini at the Opéra Comique, we could see the players urgently passing a newspaper round the orchestra during the show. The Russians had invaded Prague, and I – having just crossed the channel for the first time – I realized there were only roads between Paris and Prague. No effective natural barrier. Made an immense impression on me.

Forward to the 70s again: I auditioned my way into the class of Yvonne Lefebure, and settled down to work my way through Alfred Cortot's piano method. As I said earlier, Mme. Lefebure and I parted company after a row, but my subsequent travels round Europe were all part of the learning process. At the end of the year, I went back to London and won the fellowship that put me on the staff at the Academy.

BN: Did it feel like a distinct musical culture? You must have been working with an entirely new group of musicians, as a student and performer. Were you able to immerse yourself in that? I'm wondering whether one's listening becomes French if one moves to France, or whether internationalism works pretty much the same wherever you are, and you're always interested in whatever interests you regardless of postcode, rather than what's nearby.

DON: I had chamber music lessons with Justus Websky, whose constant refrain was 'il faut plus de personallité' – we strove to oblige, the Turkish clarinettist and the Israeli cellist and I. These nations added themselves to my experiences earlier in the summer at the Berlitz language school near the Opéra, which Rotary had sensibly decreed I attend. Our class had students from Switzerland and Austria, and an intriguingly international American who'd been born in Spain of Italian parents and worked in computing in Germany. He explained that he thought of love and family in Italian, of bodily necessities and food in Spanish, of politics in English, and of scientific matters in German. We wondered why he was learning French. And there was a young woman from Malaysia, who horrified us by explaining why you took a monkey on a picnic. The most important lesson I learnt was on the day that Mme. Hennes, our teacher, sent us off on a Round Paris Quiz. We were where the Louvre pyramid now stands, trying to find out what the 'guichets' were. 'Let's ask those English people with a Michelin guide', chorussed my friends. I looked round blankly. I could see people of every nationality under the sun, but no British ones. At last I spotted the green Michelin guide, and only after that did I actually notice the English people. They wore a particular style of clothes, but not stylishly, they wore National Health specs, and they carried a gondola basket. Manifestly English, but invisible to the one most like them. Hmmm.

As to French music, Paris was a bit disappointing. None of the singers I met wanted to sing French music – they were at a stage which England was just shaking off, where songs in their native language were sung in the accent of forty years ago, and they didn't want to sound old. I think that's a repeating cycle in every country. English student singers in the 70s found how to sing their way rather than their teachers' way, but it didn't happen in France till much later. It's probably about due to happen again in England.

So because I fell among singers in Paris, I spent a lot of time playing Schubert, and going to masterclasses with Austrian teachers – Paul von Schilhawsky, Erik Werba. I did study Debussy with Lefebure, but stupidly, I didn't go and hear Messiaen play the organ – I could kick myself. Much of my time was wasted elsewhere. Paris was the scene of a very intense final burst of trying to be a composer. I had worked out a beautiful system of composition, never been done before, and my chords had what I called valencies – it wasn't so long since Chemistry at school. And I wrote and wrote in this system, until I suddenly realized that I wasn't making any sounds that I wanted to. That's one reason I embraced arranging so keenly.

BN: What did it feel like to come back to England after that time away? Did you see the country differently? And the music scene?

DON: The year I was in Paris was the year for which Jumbo and I had won a lot of concerts in a competition. So I was constantly back and forth across the channel to fulfil these engagements. The main difference I noticed was the state of the pavements: Paris was full of incontinent dogs wandering loose.

BN: I think it can be revelatory to step away from a culture for a little while – to leave the social circuit of whatever art form you're in, and then come back after an interval and see it afresh, see it for what it is. Certain scales fall from your eyes, certain things seem more important, and so on. Did that happen for you?

DON: Not so much in Paris as during my American sojourns. But traipsing round Europe was liberating musically, mainly because I'd always been a rather diligent, even biddable, student, but now I'd had my row with Lefebure. 'I'll do it my way', became my constant rebellious thought as I walked on stage – did me no end of good.

BN: And following that period of relative isolation – I know it was quite an isolated time because you told me a good story about a Jehovah's witness once - you must have come back knowing a deal more about yourself.

DON: Yes, I was so lonely that I invited the Jehovah's Witness in. During our conversation, I wanted to illustrate some point, so I got my Bible out. He glanced at it, and handed it back, appalled. 'Mais ... mais ... c'est en anglais!' he exclaimed, and rushed away. I understood how he felt: language is important in religion. When I was the organist at the Swiss Church, I used to relish the way that Jesus turned into a different person when he went 'et alors' instead of all that 'verily, verily' stuff. You could practically smell the Gauloise and see the shrug.

Solitude taught me a lot about myself. I codified it in terrible poems, which I hope are irretrievably lost. The chief thing when I settled back into London life was that I felt like Me in a way I'd never done before, and that's a feeling that's got stronger and stronger as the years pass.

BN: I wonder whether your perception of the English and European political landscapes changed after that time as well. You've observed to me before that not enough people recall how very right wing some of the impulses of the French left were in the 60s and 70s. At this time I think you were a paid up Liberal, weren't you (if you don't mind my betraying your 70s political affiliations!) Now, I don't know whether you'd feel that one's political life affects one's work. At some level it does, because we are what we experience, and we're all exposed to so much political writing, and so many political consequences. But that doesn't mean it finds expression in the work in any direct way, of course. Having said that, though, what we're talking about with this book is a kind of political music, a deeply political music, in fact, because it's about regard for our historical inheritance, your work, I think. Amongst other things. So perhaps it would be interesting to know how you were approaching the political sphere at this early stage?

DON: I used to read *Le Monde*, and I couldn't help noticing that French politics was not at all mealy-mouthed about putting France first. Even the Communist Party seemed decidedly nationalistic. I was rather thoughtlessly liberal in my politics, as were many young students who'd been given everything on a plate. A sort of Why don't we all just get along? attitude. Reading *Le Monde* in the 70s may have made me begin to question that a little.

Being the shop-steward of NATFHE affected my politics – you can probably tell that just from my kite-flying use of the term 'shop-steward'. John Gardner and I had spent chunks of my composition lessons discussing the role of trades unions, mainly because Sir David Lumsden was wielding his new broom. Now I was Branch Secretary and it was the time of the Miners' Strike, I found myself called to endless meetings to be harangued by angry miners. The Gardner theories hadn't included this sort of thing.

Ralph Vaughan Williams is an interesting political study. No Sir Ralph for him, though he continually used his O.M. (Cunning innovation of the Establishment, that.) Always dedicated to Music for the People (his particular vision of the People), but only able to do it because of inherited wealth. (A slightly false dichotomy, I know.) In a tribute to his friend Holst, RVW mentions that though Holst was a follower of William Morris in his youth, he outgrew the 'weak points in Morris's teaching'. I admire Vaughan Williams immensely, I love his music, and no-one can doubt his sincerity – signing up for ambulance work in the War when already over the age-limit, for instance. But where, exactly, were his politics? As he said himself, 'when I am with Conservatives I become socialistic, and when I am with Socialists I become a true blue Tory'.

How politics affects a piece of music is an interesting question. My fairly recent piece *Turning Points* is an avowedly political piece because of its subject – the juddering, two-steps-forward, one-step-back, march towards democracy, seen especially through the prism of Magna Carta, Agincourt, and Waterloo, which all celebrated anniversaries in 2015. But has politics affected the actual music? Yes, first of all in the forces it employs – all sorts of choruses, from children's to community to Army Wives to choral society – then youth orchestra, children's orchestra, brass band, electric guitars, hand chimes, piano duet, organ – the lot. The musical ideas subtly adapt themselves to these groupings, so the politics of orchestration contributes to the politics of style. And the whole thing is a fantasy on a suffragist song of Sir Hubert Parry: a song political not just in subject matter, but embryonically political in musical style as well, the first of Parry's late-period political songs which defined a new sort of English tune.

BN: The other political subject I'd be interested in raising in the context of France is the war. Did you feel that legacy as a presence while you were there, thirty-odd years on? I ask for two reasons. Firstly, I think we've forgotten how profoundly the First and Second Wars are shaping our lives every day in this country, but I very much think they do. We see it less clearly than we did – there are the memorials, of course, and there are other architectural legacies, but it's all only really visible, I suppose, if you look for it. And know a bit about history, so that a visit to Stevenage or wherever has a historical context. But when I work in Germany I feel so shocked, really, by how recently this continent tore itself apart. Because city after city has no buildings predating 1950, and you can't help but see how things were reshaped, and what feels like a more distant memory in England shapes every single street there. Perhaps that's me being a bit Basil Fawlty, I don't know. But I'd be interested to know whether you had any similar experiences in France.

DON: One of the reasons I'm very glad to have been in Paris in 1968 is that the seats on the Métro reserved for the 'mutilés de la guerre' were all occupied by oldish men with one leg or none. By the time I returned, nine years later, they'd all died. But I'd seen for myself the tangible reminder of the carnage of war that France had had for fifty years, and it helped me understand the fresh flowers tucked behind the little memorial tablets to those murdered by the Gestapo as the allies closed in in 1944 – you see them everywhere about Paris. I remember chatting just a few years ago to a restaurateur in his converted butcher's shop near the Gare du Nord – it still has the wonderful tiles – about the telegrams that arrived every August, but had recently ceased, mentioning the names of those who died there in 1944. Down in the country, where Jumbo has his chateau, the massacre of civilians the same year is very much a living memory.

As you say, the same sorts of experience are on tap in Germany and Austria. It's quite daunting to visit Dresden, for instance, and walk round the museum that catalogues those who boiled to death having sought shelter in water tanks. On one of my visits to Coventry Cathedral, I was delighted to see the gilded cross destined for the restored Frauenkirche in Dresden, ready for dedication and the gift of the City of Coventry, that most under-rated gem.

BN: I mentioned that I had two reasons for wanting to ask about the war. The second was that Grandad's time in the Free French seems somehow relevant to me here. I've already mentioned how my application to Keble was paternally inflected – do you think at some level you were engaging with him when you went to France? Of course, he never really spent any time there. But I think he drove you over, didn't he.

DON: Grandad's relationship with France was a delight to him, but it was late in his life, after they'd tracked him down to pay him his pension. The actual Frenchmen he knew in the navy during the war were shadowy figures. His French was not extensive, but idiomatic to a fault. When he drove me and my things over to Paris, he was very interested in finding out something about the country those shadowy shipmates came from. But chiefly his picture of France was as the land where three of his brothers were buried.

He was similarly interested when I went to Norway to give concerts. He won his Croix de Guerre off Norway, and when they made a little grant to people who'd fought there, he was delighted to drive all the way up the west coast of Norway. Narvik was his least favourite place, though.

BN: Returning to music. At some point, you must have woken up and noticed that you'd made a transition from playing for people's rehearsals, and odd gigs in churches, and going to lectures, into getting paid, and getting your name up on posters. How did that happen?

DON: I was lucky with prizes, and they took my name here and there. The concerts with Jumbo took us both to the BBC, and a few subsequent convivial conversations set me up there as a soloist too – I gave more than 200 piano broadcasts for the BBC in just a few years, before I stopped counting. Then, when I moved from Covent Garden, I got in touch with Basil Douglas, an agent I'd done a little bit of work for, and asked him if he'd mind acting as a sort of holding address for a bit. He said that was the most refreshing way he'd been asked for representation for years, and that's how I started to work with Rampal and Larry Adler. I started to do talk-radio after a phone call from Chris Marshall, who said he hoped I was sitting down, because he was going to offer me my own show. As I've been answering your questions, I've realised how often I refer to my talk-radio work, which snowballed after the initial couple of years doing the show for Chris. Apart from its own value, it's contributed to my understanding of how most people listen to music, and how that can blend with the way I listen to music.

BN: You talked about prizes. One of those took you to Australia, and that had a profound influence.

DON: As the age of thirty approached, I started to think about various doors that were about to close. I'd never done an international piano competition. Sydney was coming up (age limit 30), so I auditioned, and became one of the forty or so lucky pianists from around the world who were flown off to Australia for a gruelling month. I took a term off from the Academy to prepare, but I couldn't cry off my concerts, so time was tight. The programmes for Sydney were very long – song recitals, chamber music, a number of short recitals with compulsory Liszt and new Australian piece, a full-length recital, and finally a Mozart concerto and a Romantic concerto. All off by heart. I chose complicated sonatas by Bax and Tippett for my long recital, and the famously lengthy Brahms One for my Romantic concerto. It became clear at an early stage of my preparation that my memory did not have room for Bax and Tippett AND Brahms and Mozart. If I could not remember Bax and Tippett I would never get to play Brahms and Mozart, so I didn't bother with the concertos at all. This strategy was all too successful. I sailed through to the finals, and was faced with the necessity of learning two concertos from scratch in five days. It can be done, but at a rather terrible cost.

The Mozart was easy to memorise. At the rehearsal, though, I hadn't had time to work out a cadenza, so I simply told the conductor how it would end (with the usual cadential trill), and then rushed back to the more challenging problems of the Brahms. Unfortunately, the next time I thought about Mozart was at the live radio broadcast. Towards the end of the first movement, the orchestra suddenly stopped playing. Only then did I remember that I should have worked out my cadenza. I began to improvise. The only guide I could come up with was the fact that the particular concerto I'd picked, the F major, went to the dominant key for the slow movement, the sharp side of the tonic key. And the development section I'd just played with the orchestra had visited the sharp keys too. So as a contrast, I started to drift to the flat keys, until I found myself in the key of C flat minor, and got stuck. How to get back to F? I trilled and arpeggiated as I dithered, when suddenly my fingers took over without my conscious volition, and showed me how, by playing the Badinerie from Bach's B minor Suite – same notes as C flat minor, but the way from B to F is easier to find. I duly concluded the movement, and pressed on into the slow movement, even as several jurors, deeply offended, left the hall.

Back in the practice room, things weren't going well. At the rehearsal on the morning of the live television broadcast, the Brahms divided itself into two. There were the bits I couldn't remember, and there were the bits I couldn't play. But in the evening, a miracle! Even when I omitted a bar in the slow movement, I merely called out, 'Don't worry, I'll stick another bar in'. The startled conductor gratefully brought the violins in at the proper place. The following morning, the *Sydney Morning Herald* carried a most perceptive review. 'David Owen Norris found himself in the position of one who grasps the hand of a friend while desperately trying to remember his name', wrote Roger Covell, adding: 'He may or may not become a famous concert pianist. He may well become something even more interesting.'

Back to the Brahms concerto. After the performance, I wept solidly for an hour, and I didn't touch a piano for six months. That was instinctive, if you like.

BN: That's extraordinary. At that stage (I'm at this stage at the time of writing, keenly aware of the pace of development when you're no longer crap but still quite green), that must have had a huge impact on you. Was it an emotional block then, you couldn't bring yourself to play? Did you think you'd play again, or were you giving up? What did you do in the mean time?

DON: I smoked a lot, watched television, and moved house after terrible squabbles with neighbours. A strange uprooted time. I didn't want to play, but I didn't think I was giving up.

BN: And how did you find your way back to the piano?

DON: After a rather protracted interval, I got back on the horse that had thrown me – that's to say, I decided to compete in the Geneva Competition.

BN: When you did sit back down, were you aware of any dissonances between the player you were and the mind that had continued developing while you weren't playing? I ask because it's often necessary to park ideas and come back to them in my trade, and sometimes that has consequences – often the idea becomes richer because you've got six months' more life to apply to it (and because, of course, the subconscious never stops working on anything, so the work usually has marinaded a bit). Sometimes you can see why you had the idea, and see that you've used it elsewhere, without realising, which can cause the idea to wither and die; and sometimes, most terrible at all, you've lost access to what you were doing. Too much has happened in your life and you're not who you were, and can't reach the core feeling out of which the idea grew in the first place. So I'm interested in whether you felt you were putting on old clothes, or whether you felt you could see new things. And how much worse had you got, technically? Had that taken a toll that had to be made up for with hours of scales?

DON: Hours of scales, certainly, and hours and hours of memorising Tchaik 1 – not going to be bitten twice, though I never got to play the concerto this time, dammit. Coming back to an idea can be a scary thing, even if it has marinaded. But coming back to the piano was not so scary – it was the same familiar piano, and the repertoire I was learning was completely different. In a small way I'd changed, but not so much as a result of silence, more as a result of Sydney.

Sydney had introduced me to a type of pianist – a type of musician – I'd never met before, the professional competitor, people who go from competition to competition, playing their competition pieces in, alas, their competition manner. Some years later, reviewing the Cardiff Singer of the World for the *Daily Telegraph*, I analysed this manner, pointing out that the most obvious way singers could set themselves apart from their rivals was to sing, not with more beauty or insight, but louder and higher, just as pianists in the same situation tried to play louder and faster. Loud and fast meant that the pianists sounded angry, loud and high, that the singers were hopelessly in love – each case an unfortunate reduction of emotional range.

It was reflecting on this sort of thing that led me to try a taste of being a professional competitor in the Geneva Competition. One juror said I was good at Adagios but less good at Allegros – if only I'd already thought of faster and louder! But I took some pride in being, I'm pretty sure, the only contestant to play an ornament in Bach, and since there were only two in the concerto finale, and since I won the Prize of the City of Geneva, I suppose I came third, kind of.

Between them, the two competitions introduced me to a new repertoire, and a new attitude to playing the piano. I didn't wholly adopt either of them. I was already forming my repertoire by sifting through what was thrown at me by the various musical worlds to which I was beginning to belong; so in Sydney I had played Byrd virginal music and Grainger folk-dance arrangements – the only Grainger in the whole competition, in his centenary year in his native country, amazingly enough. And I continued to regard the piano as a family saloon rather than a sports car – or a war-horse. But the demon pianists who play Balakirev's fiendish *Islamey*, and their almost coprophilic interest in speed, once more showed me there were other opinions than mine.

BN: I wonder whether I can ask you some specific questions about performance. What is your routine when you start to learn a piece, or get a known piece concert-ready? How do you practice?

DON: My eyes and my fingers work together well, so I can usually get close to a new piece on the first run, with enough brain left to be thinking about the possibilities as they pass. I write in necessary fingering from an early stage, always in pencil, because I'm bound to change it as I find a hand-shape that fits the phrase better. I sing a great deal to mould the phrases, though I try always to be conscious of my singing, so that I can stop when I want; because I detest pianists who sing along in concerts, like Glenn Gould. With a piece I know already, I play through very very very slowly, refreshing aural and physical memory. The two work together, but I find nowadays that the main aspect of memory is aural: I imagine the sound I want to make, and play it. This means that shape and dynamic and the actual notes are all subsumed into one process. I never memorise visually. As to practice, I have a comprehensive warm-up which lasts about an hour, and normally I'd do that about four days a week, before working on any actual music. There's not always time, unfortunately, so sometimes I do the warm-up and no music, and sometimes the other way round.

BN: And among the work that has stayed in your repertoire for a long time, have there been changes in approach? Presumably there have been changes to the way you've played them?

DON: Yes, things change – the Moonlight Sonata is still revealing new possibilities after half a century. Since I regard performance as an interaction between me and the piece and the audience, things are bound to change, even when there's no audience but me.

BN: Then on the day of a concert, is there a routine to that?

How do you approach the moment you walk onstage, do you have to deal with nerves? Britten was often sick, while Elgar apparently didn't get nervous at all, where are you along the line?

DON: I'm never nervous, not after surviving Sydney. My body subconsciously protects me on concert days by pretending to be tired, which used to bother me. But now I know I'll be full of energy once I start. So I do my full warm-up, and eat enough, and play everything through slowly. Then I just see what happens. Britten couldn't go on stage without drinking a glass of brandy, apparently, which I find astonishing. I couldn't possibly drink alcohol and still have full control.

BN: Is there an ideal rhythm of concerts? Would you like to be playing all the time if you could, or does that lead to burn-out? David Hare has it that an artist is someone who undertakes not to speak unless he has something to say, and then only to do so in conditions over which he has complete control. Which is a sort of Wittgensteinian approach, I suppose, and might be different for a performer, who isn't always minting new thoughts in the way a writer does.

DON: It's good not to be playing 52 weeks of the year. The 90s, when I more or less did that, showed me that the danger wasn't so much burn-out as staleness – slightly different. And of course, no time to do other work properly. I'm enjoying working out which half of David Hare's dictum most makes him an artist. Not speaking without something to say is always a good plan, but complete control of conditions rarely comes a performer's way. We haven't talked much about the differences between recreative artistry and pure creation. Am I the same person when I play as when I write? I must at least make Beethoven's thoughts *sound* newly minted.

BN: Do sabbatical periods play a role in the life of an artist?

DON: Very much so, unless you're the sort of artist who can always do exactly what you like. But even then, you might need to steer yourself to that variety which is the spice of life.

BN: On a related note, the theatre agent Peggy Ramsey said somewhere that she thought talent lasted ten years. A terrifying thought. I don't think it's particularly true, but I take from it the observation that artists do experience variations in intensity, besides enduring fluctuations of fashion and so on – artists do seem to have their own lunar phases. Is that something you'd agree with?

DON: It could only be true in certain bits of the theatre, including opera, where physical appearance or capability is important. So, only in recreative artistry, and by no means universally true there either. The fluctuations of artists' careers don't only depend on fashion, as you rightly observe. Kay Lawrence, who as Lady Norrington has met a lot of soloists, and who is a most sympathetic listener, told me once that nearly everyone has unlooked for, unwelcome, fallow periods of no work at all. She was far too discreet to name names, but since then I've noticed that people do disappear from time to time, and then, whoosh, they're back. That all depends on pure chance. I think of that whenever I see a flock of long-tailed tits descend on a tree to feed, picking the insects off the bark. They won't eat all the insects – they'll get nervous and fly on. If they did eat all the insects, they'd eventually die out themselves, of course. Evolutionary balance. Chance.

BN: Who were your principal collaborators at this stage in your life, when you had recovered from the Sydney competition? You were doing a lot with Jumbo as a singer; you've mentioned Trevor Hold and Bob Walker. All Northamptonshire men like yourself, although Jumbo at least you met in London rather than back home.

DON: Yes, at Nick Kenyon's party. The Northamptonshire connection went no further than those you've mentioned. I worked with lots of different musicians, more or less as a jobbing accompanist, but I boiled that down to a few regular partnerships – Jumbo, Peter Savidge, and the Viennese violinist I mentioned, Ernst Kovacic. I did concerts with the soprano Sheila Armstrong – we even did a trip to Japan – and with Dame Janet Baker, who put me into her autobiography. I made some records with the Mistry Quartet – very enjoyable. Simon Callow got in touch out of the blue the other day just to say how much he likes our Elgar Quintet, and our Bax was good too, I think.

BN: And did you start teaching at this time?

DON: I started teaching at Junior Academy on Saturday mornings, while I was still a student. I had some piano students, and I taught aural and theory. It was the theory lessons that led to my resignation. To get the students through the exam, I had to teach them how to write out ornaments – trills and mordents, and so on. But, musical notation being what it is, you can only write out ornaments very simplistically. An ornament should be like an irrational number, you can't pin them down. Yet once I'd taught a student how to write out *diddlediddlediddlediddledee*, that's how they played it. So I left that employment. By that time I was teaching at the Academy proper, harmony at first, and later aural, piano, and repertoire classes for pianists. But I found my favourite niche as a song coach, where my experiences at the Opera House, or with Dame Janet and Jumbo, or with Werba and Schilhawsky in Paris and Munich, really came in handy. I've been a song coach at the Royal College of Music too, and now I visit the Royal Northern every term, always working with singers. It's a repertoire I know backwards, and of course I love the combination of poetry and music.

BN: When did your work in radio begin? Was that part of your life from early on? How did it happen?

DON: I was a familiar sight at Broadcasting House because of all those piano broadcasts I did. Paul Hamburger, a pianist from Vienna, and a famous song coach, had moved on from staff accompanist to producer at the BBC – the Music Library is still full of scores littered with his idiosyncratic fingering, completely useless to anyone but him. Paul asked me to present a programme of my folksong arrangements. So I talked and played, and very stilted it was: I can still remember a few creaking lines from my script. But it was perhaps that sort of thing that put me into Chris Marshall's mind when he was putting together the team for *The Works*, which ran for several years. Its remit was to enquire into the whole of the musical world. We made features about everything from the song of the whale, with live links to the Antarctic, to a comparison between the effects of analogue and digital recording techniques on the chemical flow of emotion, the hobby-horse of Denis Vaughan, a Beecham pupil and Dvorak scholar who dreamed up the National Lottery. We could bring in actors from the BBC Repertory Company, so we often wrote sketches for them. For Children in Need one year we did a rather dark scene where Fafner and Fasolt, Wagner's giants from *Rhinegold*, broke into the studio looking for children to eat, but eventually donating their gold to the good cause. My favourite sketch was our riposte to a claim that the 'sound' of the universe could be represented simply by turning its radio waves into sound waves. Our rather neat commentary on that was to create the 'sound' of the rain forest by felling the trees, passing the tree-ring patterns past a supermarket bar-code reader, and treating the output as a digital signal. We played Canteloube as the outcome of this pretended process, and the studio engineer outdid us all by spending his break dubbing in the sound of chainsaws.

After *The Works* came to an end, a number of producers regularly put my name on programme ideas – most notably Elizabeth Burke. I made lots of six-programme series. *All the Rage* was one, which presented the signature songs of a decade, and eventually morphed into *Playlist*. *But I know what I like* simply asked musicians to bring along their favourite music. I would accompany them, in between asking them about it. One of those that sticks in my mind is Tony Rolfe-Johnson singing the mad scene from Britten's *Peter Grimes*, stomping round the studio in his wellies, which he'd brought to help him get in character. Then there was *Gramophones & Grooves*, produced by Andrew Green. I had one of the strangest aural experiences of my life, making that. To demonstrate how early records were made, I stood in front of a gramophone-style horn beautifully crafted in polished wood, and spoke down it to a needle quivering over a disc of warm wax. The horn was slightly larger than me. Talk about high fidelity – when they played it back it was like standing in front of myself, like an aural mirror.

I made dozens of one-off programmes: *Liszt the Virtuoso*, Tobias Matthay, the nationalist politics of the obituaries of the composers who died in 1934, Haydn's music for peculiar instruments – acres of interesting stuff which I'm really glad to know, and might never have found out any other way. Every now and again an apparently irrelevant fact will slot into place and solve some professional puzzle.

Serendipity is always a useful tool, of course, whether or not you're making radio. The grandson of the great church musician W.H. Harris lives in Andover. A few weeks ago he showed me a letter sent to his grandfather at Oxford. The letter was from the young Lennox Berkeley, and it canvassed the possibility of the University awarding Maurice Ravel an honorary D.Mus. The degree was duly awarded the following year. I've just finished reading a PhD thesis which in part explores how Berkeley made his way into influential musical circles in Paris. Quite by accident, I was able to contribute a silver bullet to the thesis.

BN: I suppose the best part of a decade passed in the environment you've been describing, different gigs, different competitions, work as an organist in Sussex, radio work, time abroad and time at the Academy. And then the big change that introduces us to the second phase of your performing career was winning the inaugural Gilmore Artist Award. Can you tell us what this was?

DON: The Gilmore is the creation of David Pocock, a quirky, polymathic American pianist who studied in Finland and Vienna, and then got a job teaching in Kalamazoo, Michigan. Kalamazoo was the home of the fabulously wealthy Upjohn Pharmaceutical companies, and of Gilmore's department store. Irving S. Gilmore was related to the Upjohns, and so, when after his death a memorial was sought, there was quite a bit of money about. The trustees approached Pocock to create a piano competition – Irving had been a keen pianist. Pocock knew the disadvantages of competitions at first-hand, so he created a 'stealth' competition. He sought secret nominations from people who knew actual working pianists, rather than professional   competitors, and then his committee tracked them round the world, listening to the candidates without the candidates knowing. As I mentioned earlier, I was nominated several times, which was lucky, because each time they checked they thought I'd gone on to do different things. But of course, I was still playing too, so eventually they bought all my records and started listening to me.

BN: And how did it come about, that you were the first recipient?

DON: Winning the Gilmore is inextricably bound up with losing *The Works*. The radio show had been taking up more and more time, and my juggling of concerts, Academy and BBC had been tricky. I asked the Warden at the Academy for an unpaid sabbatical year, which was granted. I then walked down to the BBC to tell the team the good news. They looked at me with dismay. 'You'd better go and see Drummond', said Chris Marshall, the producer. Sir John greeted me cheerily. 'Ah, I just wanted to tell you I'm axing your show', he said. 'Sorry about that'. The important thing is that I did not walk straight back to the Academy: I went home to Petworth to think, having lost all my regular income in the space of ten minutes.

It seemed a good time to try something new. I'd never crossed the Atlantic. So I got in touch with all the Americans and Canadians I'd ever met, and Roger Wright, whom I knew from his stint at the British Music Information Centre, who was running the Cleveland Orchestra. To my great surprise, a few Americans I *hadn't* met got in touch, offering me concerts here and there. This was Pocock's cunning way of saving money: instead of taking the jury to me, he had the lucky chance of taking me to the jury.

That first trip gave me an idea of the scale of North America when I decided that the 9 o'clock train from Montreal to New York was too early, and I'd do better to catch the 10 o'clock. There was, of course, only one train a day. As it dizzied above Lake Champlain (the track's like a rickety shelf tacked onto the cliff) I saw a fisherman's pick-up truck descend slowly through the melting ice. America was very different.

I managed to arrange several American trips about this time – one of them was added on to my trip to Japan with Sheila Armstrong, I remember. The odd thing about all those trips was that the planes were absolutely empty – it was the height of the first Gulf War, and we were very fearful. It's an odd experience, to be outnumbered by the cabin crew.

I first met Pocock when he knocked on the door of my hotel in New York. He had been pulling the strings all along, of course – when I saw Jim Carrey's *The Truman Show* I had a slight feeling of dèja-vu. I opened the door, and there was a man in a suit, film lights, microphones and movie cameras. 'Congratulations!' said Pocock. 'You've won'. 'Good', I replied. 'What have I won?'

In simple terms, I'd won my Bösendorfer, concerts in nearly every State in America, and the chance to pick up other jobs while I was over there – hence my summers in Ravinia, and many happy visits to advise Music Toronto.

BN: The impression I have is that you must have been performing at a very high level, to be selected. Were you aware of that, was there a sense of gathering momentum, or did it come out of the blue?

DON: Completely out of the blue. Suddenly I was swept away from my timetabling clashes between the Academy and the BBC, and presented with a completely new set of problems.

BN: What were the immediate practical implications for your work?

DON: Well, the first problem with winning a stealth competition is that you weren't keeping space for it in your diary. Even with *The Works* and the Academy disappearing completely, I'd got concerts and other broadcasts to fulfil. So for several years, as you remembered in your introduction, I was back and forth across the Atlantic like a yo-yo.

BN: This new aspect of your life took you to new places.

DON: That was wonderful! From Corpus Christi in the Gulf of Mexico to Vancouver, and amazing places in between. The beautiful panorama of the Rockies at Boise, Idaho: I played Brahms One there, and laid the ghost. Baton Rouge, where I was strolling by the Mississippi in a concert interval, all white tie and tails, when I got caught up in a riot. Police and rioters ebbed and flowed past me, completely ignoring me, except for one looter, who plonked a dozen cans of beer into my arms – I took them back to the concert hall. Detroit, where I cannily befriended a would-be mugger, a large man who tagged along with me as I walked from the Art Gallery to the station. I sized him up, and started to prattle about England. He became quite cordial, until we reached an underpass. 'This is where I usually mug people,' he said, apologetically. 'Good job we're friends,' I said. And New York, where Pocock and I celebrated so noisily after my debut that the barman complained we'd scared away the drug-dealers, and all his customers had gone home.

BN: I got caught up in a riot once, working at the Bush in 2011. I'd just led a post-show discussion, and stepped out onto the Green to see a mounted police charge break up a group of QPR and Millwall fans who were going at each other. Flares, smoke, groups of men flying apart when the horses reached them. Police horses at top speed are an extraordinary sight. To my immediate left, a police officer was addressing thirty-odd fellow officers with helmets, batons and shields, giving it the full Mel Gibson. He'd removed his helmet to shout – I assume they impede the jaw.

Setting that aside – you must have begun working with a whole new cast of people, as a result of that intensified internationalism to what you were doing?

DON: Great orchestras – Chicago, Detroit, Vancouver. Some very enjoyable chamber music with the Muir Quartet, which took me to Nashville. I've mentioned some of the singers at the Steans Institute, but I also met the visiting conductors and soloists: played piano duets with Eschenbach, jolly evenings with Zukerman and John Williams, that sort of thing. Though a good deal of my time in America was spent alone, flying from solo recital to solo recital.

BN: And were there great conductors as well?

DON: The most famous conductor I worked with was Rozhdestvensky, but we didn't click!

BN: Did your repertoire change, what was the impact on that?

DON: Repertoire was a big problem, especially the concerto repertoire. Some odd scheduling meant I had to learn both Liszts in a month for just one concert, and in the end after a huge row I cancelled the concert.

BN: Worth saying, then, it brought just as many new pressures as new opportunities – challenges of solitude, pressures of memorising, itinerance and so on? How did all that affect you?

DON: Sometimes it made me feel like two people – that's never good. From time to time it made me very angry – trapped in the machine sort of stuff. I'm not very good at being angry – I can usually see its futility. It gave me a great compassion for people who are just doing what they have to do, a tolerance of necessity.

BN: We now arrive at the crux of this book for me, the big ideological turning point in how you developed your career, and the reason I first wanted to write this. Some time in the 90s, shortly after winning the Gilmore Award, you were on the cover of Gramophone magazine. I saw a copy once, though I don't know where it is any more. And you effectively did a Prospero, and broke your staff, and ruled yourself out of tilting at a lot of the major piano repertoire that people might have expected of you, and that might have allowed you to position yourself among those 'greatest pianist in the world' types. You gave an interview in which you said that a pianist has to make a decision as to whether he wants to do the Greatest Hits, or whether he has other interests, and wants to travel in more unusual directions. And you nailed your colours at that time to the mast of English music – I guess at the time you'll have been talking about Elgar and Bax and Quilter.

This has always seemed like a pivotal moment to me. A public announcement, at the moment of your greatest influence, that you weren't sufficiently interested in the conventional pianist route to slog along it. It's occurred to me that there's a reading of that interview that suggests you were finding a way to insulate yourself from failing in a tilt at the title – it's a quality I've observed many times in myself and my brother, we both find ways to insulate ourselves from failure. It's something I fight against, creating criteria for success that mean I don't have to be brave and try really hard, because I can't actually fail. 'The play's meant to be boring so if people leave at the interval, that means it's worked', sort of thing. Redefining success until it corresponds with what happened.

But there are much less public ways of doing that than on the cover of a magazine, so I don't think that reading quite stands up. I think you really were certain that playing Rachmaninov for ever wasn't for you, and you wanted to do something else, and use the platform you'd created to advocate and interpret English music. (This is why I'm so taken aback that you think music and ideology can't mix – your entire career, in this context, is a political gesture!) This, I think, will have been tied up in where you came from, I suppose – in terms of not actually being solely a pianist. I think it also brings us back to the question of what you think music is for, and what it can do. As a writer, I spend my whole time working on things that don't exist yet, so I understand your resistance to playing the Greatest Hits for ever - the idea of endlessly reheating repertoire other people have done before is slightly deadening to me. Alice Hamilton's formulation on this front is very useful, I think. As a director, she primarily makes new plays, but will also work on a revival where the work speaks to her and, crucially, she doesn't think she'll have to wade through a lot of people's received opinions about how it ought to be done. I think that's very smart – venturing into the past where you can still engage in the act of 'making' in the present tense, and just concentrate on the play rather than think about performance context, etc. I don't know whether that resonates with you, in terms of the decision you took. What led you to conclude that you wanted to angle away from the conventional career path of the concert pianist? If you even remember the interview, perhaps it felt less emphatic than it looks from my vantage point!

DON: I gave a lot of interviews like that. It wasn't insulating myself from failure, it was a genuine statement of what I felt I was about. My attitude caused a lot of heart-searching at the Gilmore. They'd picked me because I was different, but now they needed me not to be as different as all that.

First, as to failure: England's musical culture is predominantly choral and vocal, so we all have a basic knowledge of what singing should sound like. America's musical culture is based on the piano, and they all know what pianos should sound like. I was staggered to find that American audiences (and critics) can make a judgment on a pianist from a single note. My first American reviewers were confused by me. They invariably enjoyed the concert, but they felt they shouldn't have done, because I didn't play the piano 'well' enough. This is a really interesting situation, unless it's you who's at the centre of it, and then it's terrible. I had to do something about it.

I'd studied technique very thoroughly with Yvonne Lefebure in Paris. I'd worked on it deeply myself, inventing new exercises. I'd added really difficult pieces to my repertoire, and I'd done pretty well in competitions, not just those international ones. Audiences loved my concerts. Yet now, here were critics who'd listen to my first chord, and sigh, even if they stayed and enjoyed. So I started again. I worked all through Alfred Cortot's *Rational Principles of Piano Technique* for the second time. I invented still more new exercises. I practised technique for hours and hours. And this time, I listened to myself with those critics' ears, trying all the time to keep my own ears too: what's the point of perfect diction if you've nothing to say?

It worked. American reviewers even began to comment on my technique, while still enjoying the music. I'm rare living proof that you *can* improve your piano technique after the age of forty. But the repertoire difficulties still remained. Purely from a commercial point of view, the standard repertoire was problematic. There are a lot of very good pianists who play it just fine. Quite a lot of it, it so happened, I didn't play at all. If you know great chunks of the song repertoire by heart, if you wake from a recurring dream to discover you are indeed in sober fact playing *Here comes the bride* again, it's less likely you've had time to memorise all 32 Beethoven sonatas. No point playing catch-up. Anyway, my musical tastes having formed in the way they did, I didn't even like some of the standard repertoire. I agree with Alice Hamilton's philosophy, that the only point of re-hashing something is if you've got a unique ingredient to add; but I don't worry too much about received opinions. Here it's easiest to point to Beethoven's Moonlight Sonata, which I play a lot, in ways entirely my own – at least, I've never heard anyone play it like that, and my audiences always tell me that neither have they. Los Angeles mainly hated it twenty-five years ago, though one critic saw the point. These days, people always seem to love it, which could be the reward for just staying alive, and therefore attaining at least the appearance of maturity. More likely the reading has improved – in fact, just yesterday in the car I solved a problem of scansion in the second movement which I've been struggling with for about fifty years.

Back to nineties America. The difficulty was that my own repertoire hadn't yet reached a point of focus. I sometimes think, with incredible ingratitude, that if the Gilmore hadn't come along when it did, I might have become what I think I've become about a decade earlier. As it was, the nineties were a turbulent whirl, apart from that very important technical improvement.

BN: As a result of your concert career developing, every other aspect of your work also took a leap forward at this time. Your radio work in particular.

DON: It was in the middle of all this that I became one of the team of presenters for Radio 3's drive-time show, *In Tune*. My involvement varied – for a while, I broadcast from London, then later, I was Mr. Birmingham about once a month, and later still I did outside broadcasts from festivals with live audiences, often sitting at a piano myself, talking – something I try to make a bit of a trademark.

BN: And you've already mentioned that you spent some time directing festivals.

DON: During the seven years in the 80s and early 90s when I directed the Petworth Festival, I applied my social ideas – my ideology – about music-making and society. This was only partly because it had got into debt. I would invite my student Paul Murphy, now conductor of the Birmingham Royal Ballet, to put together an orchestra from the Academy, which would come down in a coach for a mad weekend doing a piece they'd know and love, but probably hadn't played much – so they really wanted to come. We started with Holst's *Planets*, with me doing the fade-out women's choir on a synthesizer. We did Tchaik 4, and the Ravel Piano Concerto. By the time we got to Beethoven Nine, the church choir (with some augmentation) was accomplished enough to tackle it. Academy chamber musicians came down too, staying with local families, of course. I noticed that even making the sandwiches for the orchestra led to a much greater involvement in actually *listening* to the music at the concerts – I don't just mean that the helpers came, they *wanted* to come much more, and they got more of the music's message – or what I take to be the music's message, anyway! We did the

Schubert Octet in café format, with tables and beer, offending some of the Festival stalwarts, and delighting others. Our finances returned to health, and South East Arts had to suggest new ways we might require subsidy, since they wanted to be associated with us, but we weren't losing enough money. The happy coincidences of Sussex meant that two successive Arts Ministers were local MPs – Richard Luce and Tim Renton. They came along with great enthusiasm – very helpful.

Then Michael Tearle got in touch, wanting programme ideas for his Cardiff Festival. I was Artistic Director there for three or four years, picking up some other Cardiff-based jobs as a result – I mentioned that television quiz. But Welsh politics changed, and Michael retired. Good while it lasted.

BN: Around this time, you did start making forays into composition again – I'm thinking of *Die! Sober Flirter*, which you made for the radio.

DON: I still perform *Die! Sober Flirter* from time to time. Elizabeth Burke was producing *Table Talk* for Radio 3, and she rang to see if I could think of anything a quarter of an hour long, food-related, to mark the Mozart Bicentenary. I'd just been doing Rimsky-Korsakov's chamber opera based on Pushkin's poem *Mozart & Salieri* for the Brighton and the Petworth Festivals, and I thought up an amusing reversal of fortune based on the legend that Salieri poisoned Mozart. *Die! Sober Flirter* as title was thought a joke too far for the radio audience, so it went out first as *Die Zabaglione*. But the phrase 'Die! Sober Flirter' is the pivot of the plot, so the original title is now always restored. The musical conceit of the piece is that it's a Mozart piano concerto, except the piano is replaced by a harpsichord, the orchestra replaced by oboe, viola and double-bass, and three singers are added, partly to carry the plot, of course, but partly to perform the cadenzas. Since the plot explored what might have happened if Mozart had not died in 1791, I adopted a style of Mozart-Plus. This meant the question of musical language was settled from the start, and I could concentrate on what I was going to say with it – a valuable lesson which bore fruit when I had time, ten years later.

I wrote two other pieces in the nineties. One was a commission to end a music competition with something for everyone to join in – flute quartet, clarinet quartet, mezzo soprano and guitar, piano solo, and harpsichord and viola da gamba tuned a quarter-tone flat. I wrote a libretto round *Beauty and the Beast*, and the music was a set of variations on *When I survey the wondrous cross* – that fairy tale always seems like a parable. I called it *The Cost of Living*. The flutes represented Beauty, the clarinets, the Beast, and so on. The performance was a disaster, of course – everyone had been too busy rehearsing their competition pieces to bother with this new thing. I found the score just the other day when I was clearing the attic. Not bad, I think. Must see if I can re-do it for a more rational selection of instruments.

BN: It's a good title, that's half the battle!

DON: It is, isn't it! The other piece was a setting of Brian Patten's poem *Interruption at the Opera House* for Petworth. This was great fun, with parodies of Ives and Stockhausen, and parts for the Petworth band, the various choirs, the handbell ringers, my children's choir (in nightcaps), and a small orchestra. Doubt if I'll revive that one, though.

BN: Usually work written in the voices of others, then, from what you're saying? And work occasioned by others, rather than yourself?

DON: Yes. These few pieces from the nineties were generally very anonymous. I snatched at opportunities, which were usually the wrong opportunity, instead of making time to do what I wanted to do.

BN: This brings us back, I think, to the conversation around ideology. The trying on of voices here seems to me to be in part a trying on of ways of seeing, ways of speaking.

DON: I hadn't yet realised that the key to saying what I wanted to say was to write in a language I understood.

BN: But composition can't be said to have come back to the fore for you. As there was so much going on, the focus was still performance, not writing.

DON: Yes, a great deal going on. I might have been wiser to have had a plan, but I was in what seemed to be uncharted and unchartable waters, and planning was difficult. It wasn't till the welter died down that I was able to digest what had happened. I'm still working out how to incorporate some of the experiences of twenty-five years ago into my work.

At a particularly tempestuous time in the late nineties, when I really needed some firm ground, I got a fellowship at the University of Southampton, part of a new AHRC scheme to expand practice-led research. Some thinking-time at last! In 2000 I recorded two CDs that I regard as the foundation of my 'real' performing career. One was on square piano. No-one had taken the eighteenth-century square quite so seriously before. I showed that the World's First Piano Concertos had been composed expressly for this tiny instrument. The other was on modern piano – the complete piano music of Edward Elgar. At last, two strands of my performing work had found a considered focus: early keyboards, and English music. I'd been working away at such things for ever, of course, but piecemeal.

BN: So those records, produced out of your work at Southampton, felt like really gathering together what you were all about into a statement for the first time? They were your emergence from all the buffeting activity you've described into a sense of having a clear identity and a project?

DON: Exactly that. Most uncharacteristically, when they came out, I thought 'Well, now I can die happy'.

BN: How would you summarise the argument, the image put forward by those two records, when considered as a single gesture, as you've just presented them?

DON: The thing they have in common is that they express things I had come across in the normal course of my musical life – important things – that had captivated my interest. For instance, I'd gone to the Cobbe Collection (of composer-related keyboard instruments) to make a radio programme, and Alec Cobbe, whom I already knew well, showed me his latest acquisition, a Zumpe square piano, signed by JC Bach. There were many intriguing aspects to this instrument, but the one that particularly struck me was the damping mechanism, two hand-levers, one raising the dampers from middle C up, the other, from middle B down. You couldn't 'change the pedal', as it were, until you had a hand free, and it occurred to me that this cumbersome mechanism must have demanded ingenuity from composers. I mentioned this at a dinner party the following day, wishing I had a square piano to experiment on, and a fellow guest immediately said 'Have one of mine'. It fitted perfectly into the back of my 2CV (you can get anything in the back of a 2CV), and I used the instrument to make the discoveries embodied in my record: not only how ingenious the composers became in the face of the cumbersome mechanism, but also the existence of a cache of piano concertos published in London in the 1770s. These were mainly by German musicians, many attached to the Court – J.C. Bach and Abel, for instance – but also including some breezy works by James Hook. The earliest of them all, published in 1769, was by Philip Hayes, who became Heather Professor at Oxford in succession to his father, William (who built the Holywell Music Room). Hayes taught the spinet to his fellow undergraduate, James Woodforde, and the parson's diary contains a vivid account of their carousing when they learned of the fall of Quebec – such carousing that it's no surprise that Hayes became the Fattest Man in England. I've got a rubber stamp somewhere that says: The World's First Piano Concerto was written by the Fattest Man in England. You'll have spotted that many aspects of the story fit snugly into my own life. And I was able to record the music on the instrument that pointed me in the right direction, at the Cobbe Collection.

Its companion record, the Elgar, likewise had a special angle.

My friend John Norris (not my brother) was very keen that I should record coherent versions of the improvisations that Elgar recorded on hot wax, but never wrote down. So I learned them by ear, and in the few places where Elgar had fumbled, I tidied them up. John also wanted me to investigate the Concert Allegro, so I went to the British Library to look at the manuscript. Elgar had crossed out about a third of it – not a coherent chunk, but a bar here, a few bars there. Briefly, there were clues in the manuscript that this was because Fanny Davies, the great pupil of Clara Schumann who had requested the piece, not being acquainted with Elgar's style, had played it too slowly. When the reviews said the piece was much too long for its material, Elgar did not draw the obvious conclusion. (He didn't actually meet Fanny till the late 1920s, by the way, and never heard her play it.) He assumed it was actually too long, and the way he went about shortening it tells you a lot about how he put it together in the first place. In fact, the shortenings were not necessary at all, and so, buoyed up by the thorough knowledge of Elgar's piano-playing that reproducing the Improvisations had given me, I recorded the complete original, plus a few wistful pencillings that Elgar, unable to believe he could have been quite so wrong, had added actually to *lengthen* some sections. I play this magnificent piece a lot, and it always works perfectly, as you might expect of Elgar at the height of his powers. Incidentally, I don't ever play the shortened travesty, which is the only version in print – complete with misreadings of a perfectly clear manuscript. That's the version John Ogdon recorded.

BN: What else did you learn about Elgar, gathering the complete piano music together like that?

DON: Apart from those technical pianistic things, I learnt a lot about his personality. There's a note at the end of one of his piano manuscripts: 'I know this ends in the wrong key'. I love that! I imagine him speaking rather testily. His recorded improvisations show a great musician ignoring unimportant blemishes, and concentrating on his message: an admirable fixity of purpose. This sense of purpose he would modulate slightly when interacting with others (as when he shortened the Concert Allegro). When he sent his Piano Quintet off to Novellos, he appealed to the publisher's reader for help in writing down what he called his 'tadpole' and 'straddlebug' passages. Harold Brooke's solutions, though accepted by the composer, are rather staid. I think these were originally improvised passages, and I sometimes bend them in performance, bearing in mind what Elgar said to Compton Mackenzie about his piano-playing when refusing the latter's request that he record the piece: 'it would madden with envy all existing pianists'. He immediately deflated this magnificent boast by adding 'I never did play, really'. But, having followed his fingers so far, I feel I know what he was boasting about.

BN: Then there's the record you made containing his first sketch for the Cello Concerto theme, and his last song, *XTC*, which I think no one had recorded before. And a song called *Sabbath Morning At Sea,* which has the most amazing opening phrase – which might be worth coming back to when we talk about the opening phrase of your Piano Concerto.

DON: Yes, that was a later stage of my Elgar explorations, recorded at the Cobbe Collection again on Elgar's own square piano. Rifling through the BL's manuscript collections again, I established that the original version of the song-cycle *Sea Pictures* was for soprano and piano, which explained a few things that had been puzzling me. Clara Butt, who sang the premiere (with orchestra) had a low voice, but the original version of the last song had a top B at the end. This is because the first and last songs were both in the key of E, which was a way that Edward Elgar (E.E. – he sometimes called himself The Octave) signed himself into his works. In the end, the last song was brought down to D – but it seemed to me that the resulting top A at the end would still be pretty problematic for a contralto. Then I found Sir Edward German's obituary tribute to Elgar in 1934. 'I first met Sir Edward in Norwich,' he wrote. 'He was conducting his *Four Sea Pictures*.' But there are five of them! Then I found the photograph of the rehearsal in St. Andrew's Hall. Only two people are not looking at the camera, a nondescript violinist, and Elgar, who is scowling in the most ferocious manner at Clara Butt. I think Clara never sang the last one at all!

Anyway, you're right about the opening phrase of *Sabbath Morning at Sea*, which is in fact the coda from a little polka he wrote for his first fiancée years before – Helen Weaver, who left him to go to New Zealand, apparently to die of tuberculosis, except that the excellent climate allowed her to recover. She absolutely haunts his music. The late Brian Trowell had a theory that the Cello Concerto is all that's left of a lament for Helen's son Kenneth Munro, whom he thinks Elgar met in London while Kenneth was in between combat in the Dardanelles and death on the Somme. The original sketch of the famous theme is entitled '?'.

BN: Allow me to digress briefly, and enter an observation in the historical record here. Shortly after hearing of Munro's death, Elgar became ill with debilitating toothache. He had an operation in the Acland hospital in Oxford – which is now part of Keble, our college – and it was upon coming round from the operation that the first theme of the Cello Concerto apparently came to him. I'd just like anyone interested in that piece to go and listen to the bells of St Giles along the road, and within earshot at that time before the ubiquity of the motor car, when they ring, and speculate for as long as the bells sound as to where that opening theme stemmed from. Hint dropped!

Returning to this second record – you also included the *Dream of Gerontius* piano transcriptions on it, I think? These are another favourite recording of mine.

DON: Yes. Elgar transcribed the beginning and the end of his great piece, the Prelude and the Angel's Farewell. The most memorable performance I've ever given of them was in Broadmoor. The patients I met were quite heavily sedated, but this piece brought them alive in the most astonishing way. I was playing an upright piano, and half-way through I happened to glance round, and where there had been dull, hooded eyes, there was suddenly gleaming comprehension. As you know, Elgar worked in a mental hospital, the Powick Asylum, and I wondered whether he knew something about communication that can only be found out that way.

BN: Has the identity you found through those records remained central to your work?

DON: I think I found a focus that I've been able to maintain.

I've moved on from Elgar (whom I still perform a lot of course) to Hubert Parry and Lambert and Walton. And I've moved on from the square piano to the 1820s Broadwood grand. I keep finding fascinating things that'll take ages to explore. For instance, getting on twenty years ago, Barry Sterndale-Bennett showed me a manuscript from his ancestor's library (William Sterndale Bennett, Mendelssohn's friend). It was a score showing the flute, violin and cello 'accompaniments' to Mozart's C major Piano Concerto K.467, in the hand of J.B. Cramer, dated 'Munich 1836'. Cramer had published his adaptation of that concerto ten years before, but every library in the world has lost the instrumental parts, and there was no score. Now, thanks to that discovery, we could play the original, and properly explore the changes Cramer made to the piano part. As I write, I'm preparing at last to record it.

It was in the new millennium that my media work gained focus too. I began to present *Building a Library*. I do one or two of these every year. I did a couple of good things in John Bridcut's remarkable television programmes on English composers. And it was at this moment of comparative calm, as my fiftieth birthday approached, that I found the motivation to make myself a composer once again.

On the 11th September 2001, I was in Ayr with Philip Langridge, about to perform a programme of songs from the Great War. Philip rushed into my room with news of the Twin Towers attacks. Old War meets New War, it seemed as we watched, and it was a sombre concert that night. A number of things came together in my mind, and the next morning, as we waited for our cancelled planes, I conceived a song-cycle for tenor, cello and piano – Philip's daughter Jennifer was in our programme too. I chose two poems by Sassoon, Brooke's *The Soldier* (which gave me the cycle's title, *Think only this*) and McCrae's *In Flanders Fields*. It seemed to me that such well-known words needed a conventional melodic style – the sort of tune, in fact, that might have been composed at the time they were written. This decision gave me the same permissions (or freedoms, rather) that I had enjoyed in *Die! Sober Flirter*. But the accompaniment, and especially the possibilities offered by the cello, could enjoy different freedoms. The musical language that resulted seems to delight audiences, and it's a piece that gets played a lot. *Think only this* showed me how to create a rich language that's recognisably my own, and it's that language that I've developed in each piece since then. I'm not claiming ownership of this blending process, of course – Britten did it all the time, I've noticed subsequently – but I'm glad I stumbled upon it. Stumbling is just occasionally a more fruitful process than working things out in advance.

BN: This takes us up to the threshold of the third movement of this book, a discussion of your work as a composer, so perhaps we'll pick up the cues in what you've written about *Think only this* momentarily, and return to conclude this general, wide survey of your working life as a musician. Getting on for two decades after you found your way back to composing, you're still at Southampton, and still performing, and still working on the TV and the radio.

DON: Luckily enough, that's right. I feel fulfilled in a way that had always escaped me, though just at present, as a number of long-mulled performing things come to a head, I'm aware that

I must make still more time for composing.

BN: Your specialism in the field of early pianos, which seems to have developed and found its voice as a result of your time at Southampton, is now much in the ascendant, in terms of what you think about and write about and play.

DON: Early pianos are leading me to some really interesting ideas, ideas that don't crop up at the more self-sufficient modern instrument: in particular, how composers used dynamic signs to notate rhetorical alterations to the tempo. I've been developing that thought since 2008, and I often present my ideas in academic contexts. At present, I'm mulling over how best to bring the information to the people that really need to know – sixth-formers and music students, as well as music-lovers. Another aspect of early pianos I'm investigating is the divided damper rail. I first discovered this in the eighteenth-century square piano. One of the happy accidents of arriving to live in Andover was to get to know Ian Caddy, another of that great crop of English baritones my age, whom I'd never yet met. Ian lives up on Andover Down, and he owns a Broadwood grand with the divided damper rail. The sustaining pedal is simply sawn in two – very convenient. He very kindly hired it out to me at Southampton, and I set about seeking clues to the divided pedal's use in music. Beethoven certainly tried it out in Op.109 (Broadwoods sent him a very similar piano), and there are traces of it all over Mendelssohn, whose aunt had a Broadwood. This was so encouraging that I persuaded Peter Newham, who makes extraordinary and beautiful pianos, to adopt the device, and it was Peter's piano that I demonstrated at the Academy, and which I used to open the Broadwood Archives at the Surrey County Record Office. Eventually I acquired my own Broadwood with divided pedal, and that's recently led me to the discovery that Cramer actually positioned his pedal markings to show you which half of the pedal to press down. There's a lot to find out still about the period of the most popular classical music, roughly from Haydn to Brahms, not least those piano-tuning temperaments I mentioned, which persisted much longer than most people think, and which change the sound of the music entirely. So while I'm glad I still play modern pianos, I'm pleased I've got so deeply into the older ones.

BN: That development, of course, has influenced your repertoire once again, and brought other things into focus.

DON: A beautiful antique piano is the star of the show in a way that a modern piano can never be. Audiences crowd round it, greedy for information. It reminds you that there's more to listening to music than listening to music; that people are interested in all sorts of things at once. And early pianos decorate my excursions into a domestic nineteenth-century repertoire that's interesting but would sound a bit simplistic on modern instruments. All the Jane Austen-related music that I play from time to time at Chawton House, where she used to visit her brother; the Tennyson songs composed by none other than Edward Lear, which I've just recorded for Harvard – Tennyson preferred these to all others; Edward Loder's settings of Isaac Watts, which Southampton students performed to mark the recent bicentenary; Dickens's opera, which we put on at the Nuffield; music perhaps not strong enough to appeal across the years without its charming period dress.

BN: What do you think it was that took your attention back into the history of the instrument, and the repertoire around that?

DON: Chance again. Visiting Alec Cobbe the day after he'd got his new square; that generous fellow guest at the dinner party; Ian Caddy's Broadwood happening to be in Andover; having an academic appointment where playing early instruments counted rather more than playing modern ones (unless you were playing new music, of course); coincidences of that sort. Mind you, that sort of coincidence happens all the time – the trick is to take advantage of them. I'd been working on early pianos since 1984, when David Wilson-Johnson and I made the first recording on an early piano of Schubert's *Winterreise*. But things didn't come together in a big way until fifteen years after that first recording.

BN: The question of historical practice is also a musical minefield, isn't it. There are people like Norrington who are very committed to it. I don't know where you stand on all that – to an extent, the basis of your work now is that knowing exactly how things were done is important?

DON: I like to know how pieces were played at various periods. I can try playing Mozart on a Mozart-style fortepiano, or I can play arrangements from the 1820s on the much bigger pianos of the 1820s. And now there are those who study how Mozart was played in the 1890s or the 1930s. All very interesting, but to carry conviction, performers need to absorb these historical ways so completely that it seems to be the only way possible for them. So these days, I play Mozart in only two ways – the 1820s way, or out on a limb on a modern piano, just seeing what comes out of everything I know. Beethoven works well like that as well.

I never play Bach on the piano these days, except in proper, considered, piano transcriptions. If I want to play original Bach, I find an organ or tune my clavichord, because the piano's power of differentiating individual notes is too tempting, and leads you into all sorts of problems. My interest in transcriptions is worth explaining. Ever since I got into Arnold Bax's music, I'd known about the *Bach Book for Harriet Cohen* that OUP published in 1932, after Harriet had cajoled a Bach transcription from a dozen British composers. During a talk on Bach I gave at Symphony Hall in Birmingham, I bewailed the fact that Harriet's transcriptions had gone out of print. A hand went up in the audience. It was OUP's music director, and straight away he arranged to reprint, not just that book, but another volume bringing together a selection of the Bach transcriptions published individually by the founding director of OUP's Music Department, Hubert Foss. (As it happens, Foss's daughter Diana lives in Southampton, where we've become good friends – happy chance!) I supplied a Preface to each book, and I'm proud of my role in their reappearance. They helped revive my interest in transcription, and as well as digging out my old Joni Mitchell pieces, I polished up Walton's *Spitfire*, and made my own versions of all six of Elgar's *Pomp & Circumstance* Marches, which I recorded along with Karg-Elert's version of Elgar's *Falstaff*. It was playing Karg-Elert's transcription of the First Symphony at the Wigmore that began my immersion in Elgar, you'll recall. Most recently, in the light of a colloquium on musical meaning that we held at Southampton, I've made a cumulative set of transcriptions of the Scene of the Cold Genius from Purcell's *King Arthur*, with the dual purpose of demonstrating how meaning can be added to music, and also providing a great opener for my piano recitals. It segues seamlessly into *The Spitfire*, and the two pieces together act as a good introduction to who I am and what I do.

Returning to the question of historically informed performance, I recently learned that Vaughan Williams used to object to the use of harpsichords in Bach because the very sound of it gives the music 'an antiquarian flavour that we want to avoid at all costs'. Put all these considerations together, and what have you got? Just yourself, and your confidence and your musicality, informed by as much knowledge as you can bring to bear, but not all of which you can incorporate. And you have your audience, whom you can let in on your thoughts exactly as much or as little as you want, through speaking or through programme notes. I sometimes think of performance as a conspiracy between the performer and the audience, sometimes even at the expense of the composer. The paradox is that as I get deeper into 'authenticity' I realize that the most important authenticity is my own.

BN: What were the long-term consequences of your decision to shape your image away from the classic solo recital repertoire? You've said there's a world in which the Gilmore delayed your development into who you are now, so I sense that you see what's happened since you gave all those interviews as a positive thing – but can you outline a little how it affected your work?

DON: The long-term consequence is that Roger Covell's

Sydney prediction is in part fulfilled. My life is much richer and more interesting than if I'd simply got stuck in the mad busy-ness of the 90s: more interesting for me, but also, I think, more interesting for my audiences. It made it harder to get work for a time, while people were wondering quite what I was – but they wondered that before the Gilmore too. I chatted about this difficulty with a friendly PR person once. 'You do too many things', she said. 'Give something up'. But I didn't want to give anything up, not altogether anyway; and these days enough people seem to have worked out what I am to keep me in audiences. It's the range of the things I do that prompts me to do them in the way I do.

BN: Are there things you look back on now from the span of your performing career, and indeed your broadcasting career, and feel particularly proud of?

DON: I'm proudest of things that I do in my own particular way. Broadcasting-wise, everything I've learned over thirty years comes together in my *Chord of the Week* slots. The videos I've just made for the LSO apply the same techniques to a longer slot, and I think surpass the thing I did for John Bridcut about Parry's *Jerusalem*. There was a time when I feared that I could never do anything better than that, but now I think I have. Performances – well, the run-through concerts for this recording of Mozart adaptations from the 1820s have been pretty spectacular, so I have high hopes that (as I always think) the best is yet to come. Performances that stick out in my mind at present are of the Moonlight Sonata: in Jumbo's concert hall in France, with a full moon shining in, last summer; on Christopher Barlow's Schantz copy in Frome last month – the first time I've ever been able to obey the continuous pedal mark absolutely literally, all the way through. The audiences were as pleased with those performances as I was. You'll observe that I think I'm continuing to improve! It's always either the latest thing or the next thing that I'm proudest of. My older performances, I tend to think, could and should have been better, however well they went down at the time.

BN: I feel as well that we should touch briefly on the years and years you and I spent working on *Winterreise*, which might not loom large for you, but was crucial to my own artistic development, and was, I think, a product of your long relationship with the Dartington Festival.

DON: *Winterreise* is central to my music-making, the piece I've performed more than any other, in more ways. As I've said, Jumbo and I recorded it back in 1984, in the poet's order rather than Schubert's happenstance order (long story). We performed it a lot that way, always on early pianos. About the same time, I gave the first complete performance since Liszt himself of Liszt's transcriptions of twelve of the twenty-four songs. I played those transcriptions everywhere, all round Europe and America. When I got together with Philip Langridge, he wanted to sing *Winterreise*, and we did it in Schubert's order, mainly on early pianos. Then Sir John Tomlinson asked me to accompany him singing the piece, on modern piano. And finally, I've accompanied Thomas Guthrie in it several times, Tom singing while manipulating a remarkable puppet, on a lighted stage-set with projected film – the singer out of the light and wearing black gloves, of course. An extraordinary experience, and probably not the one single way one would want to hear the piece, but a wonderful supplement to the other ways. Dartington was the sort of place where you could spend time doing that – and then of course, you put the show on yourself in the Tristan Bates Theatre in Soho.

BN: Oh, the glamour! I've just always loved spending time with the piece. Next time I've got pull at a theatre, I'll get you to give it another spin.

What are the other pieces that have meant most to you? The music you've been most grateful to be able to perform, and the work that has been important?

DON: Besides the pieces that have cropped up continually throughout this memoir – lots of Elgar, Beethoven's Moonlight – there's Brahms's Op.118. I'll never get to the bottom of those. Haydn's big E flat Sonata. Mozart K.467. Poulenc's *Les soirées de Nazelles*, and his Flute Sonata. Constant Lambert's Piano Sonata and Concerto for Piano and Nine Players. Bax's Viola Sonata. Sterndale Bennett's *Maid of Orleans* Piano Sonata.

BN: Can I ask you what you think music has lost and won in the time you've been playing? What has disappeared that you regret, or celebrate not dealing with any more? And what are the things you have now that you're grateful for?

DON: The most obvious change to me is that fewer people can read music or play the piano a bit than when I was a child. Very few people whistle tunes any more – that may be connected with pop's changing attitude to melody. People still sing quietly as part of their lives, but they're usually 'singing along' with a radio: all rather passive. The decline in musical literacy is very serious. It confines would-be musicians to aural transmission, which on its own is prescriptive, inefficient and imprecise. Musical notation confines its precision to just a few clearly defined things. Everything else (within traditional reason) is up to the performer – a useful freedom. It's hard to retain that freedom if you learn things from a recording. Music students these days often get to know a piece by listening to it on YouTube, rather than reading it through – and they rarely notice just whose performance it was! The danger is that almost without realizing it, they'll adopt the speed or the tone or the detail of the phrasing. It's not just students, of course. I spent a day once with a quite famous young American pianist, who explained that he took the various details of his interpretations from all the recordings that he liked. I asked whether he ever worried that the performing decisions he copied from different recordings might be incompatible, but he didn't understand what I meant. And when I asked if he ever tried thinking about the pieces for himself, he laughed and said 'Why reinvent the wheel?' Even when a composer records his own music – Elgar or Stravinsky or Britten, say, all of whom produced excellent recorded performances of most of their important pieces – that doesn't mean that their notations can never be interpreted in a different way, as becomes very clear when they themselves recorded something twice. As to inefficiency – suppose you need to know whether a piano sonata is too hard for you. You can flick through the score in about a minute, or you can sit and listen for half an hour, and still not be sure. And as to imprecision, very few people can hear everything that's going on, even after repeated hearings. Fine, that young American's listeners may not realize the dislocation between Rubinstein's speed and Horowitz's phrasing: fine, the illiterate's audience may not notice the notes added or omitted. But just as we worry about ordinary literacy, I worry about musical literacy. I haven't even mentioned sight-reading. How can you make a living in music if you can't sight-read? Of course, illiterates often have very fine memories, but to me the disadvantages outweigh the advantages.

Funny how attitudes to memorisation fluctuate. Mozart would play from a blank sheet of paper rather than abandon the practice of the day, which was to play from the copy. In the 1850s, Sterndale Bennett gave the premiere of his Sonata Duo (cello and piano) with an empty score before him – he only got round to writing it out *after* the concert. It was Clara Schumann and Liszt who changed all that, playing from memory with no copy in sight. I think they were trying to communicate the fact that, even when it was Beethoven, say, who had actually written the music, they had made it so much their own that it was as if they had written it too: it was their way of owning it. Sviatoslav Richter ended up giving his recitals with anglepoise lamp and page-turner, even in Chopin studies that he'd played for ever. I find a greater freedom when I play from memory, but there isn't time to memorise everything.

Playing the piano a bit – or anything a bit, or singing in a choir – gives you extra ways to appreciate what's going on. Every subtle listener I've ever met has been able to do something musical themselves, even if they're nowhere near professional. So the thing I welcome most in modern musical culture is the huge growth in choral singing – mainly quite informal singing at present, and often illiterate (and wonderfully memorised), but it may eventually feed into more formal sorts of choral music. It'd be good if we could do something similar with piano playing. Einaudi's made a start!

BN: I came across a striking piece of invective from Yehudi Menuhin in an interview the other day, that feels worthwhile mentioning while we're on this subject. Menuhin did a book of interviews with Robin Daniels, who asked him about pop music. The answer ran:

Pop music, when it originates spontaneously, in the back streets of Liverpool, as with the Beatles, or on the wrong side of the tracks in a city in California – this I am all for. Pop music degenerates when it becomes heavily commercialised, has little musical content, and appeals only in a compulsive, hypnotic way, feeding the desire of a large group of people to blot out everyday thoughts and cares. The senses are then horribly battered, and for a time the audience are no longer balanced, moderate human beings.

He goes on to describe attending a rock gig and having to leave because it reminded him too much of the Nuremberg rallies, and he felt alarmed seeing young people put in that frame of mind (or mindlessness).

I mostly listen to music that would broadly be categorised as 'pop', but I think he's probably bang on. The stuff I hear in the gym or on the radio very much fits his description. However, you've been a little more respectful – so is there perhaps some snobbery from Menuhin here? I remember Linda Bassett telling me about the time she went to see the Beatles, and thinking she'd be above all the screaming everyone seemed to do in films of their concerts. Then seeing them walk on stage, and screaming her lungs out till they walked back off at the end of the set. There is a drugging that goes on with effective pop music, isn't there?

DON: I think Menuhin has forgotten that music *is* a drug. Like alcohol, it can be enjoyed intellectually – you can relish the vintages and the terroir, you can match a wine to a food, you can even collect the labels. But you can also get drunk. I would find it easy to think, like Menuhin, that music should not be a drug, because heaven knows, I collect the labels! But I try never to forget that the vast majority even of classical music listeners are not fully engaging their minds, they're letting the sound of the music have its effect upon them. And that, I suspect, is how music became important to us as a species – a decorative art was put to significant uses, in the temple, on the hunting field, the battle-field, on the stage. And its importance was through its sheer sound, rather than what the sound *meant*. Trumpet-calls mean something to an infantryman. To a poet, they're just 'martial'. Which of them most enjoys the sound of the trumpet? Intellectual meaning in music is something extremely sophisticated, and no-one should be chided for not getting it. Those of us who try to find ways of coding our meanings into music mustn't forget the drug aspect.

Back to what's changed. You might expect me to welcome how easy it is these days to listen to whatever music you like, but I find myself partly agreeing with Lambert and Walton and Britten, all of whom expressed fears that broadcasting would cause people to listen only casually to music in the background, not giving it the concert-hall attention the composer had banked on when writing it. Many pieces of classical music save up their surprises. Modern listening habits require something different: 'in today's programme, jolly interesting Z, amazing Y, and fairly appealing X. But first ...'. Of course, I'm full of the usual hypocrisy here: 'Spotify's all right for *me*, because I don't listen to things in that way'. Useful resource, of course it is.

I miss the chaotic music shops. When I was a student in London, there were a dozen I used to visit regularly. Some of them still survive, but computers mean that they all know what stock they've got, for a start. They all used to be very well differentiated, according to the taste of the manager: Cramers in St. Martin's Lane was presided over by Mr. De'Ath, who knew everything. There were Boosey & Hawkes, Chappell's, UMP, Universal, Schott's, and Novello's: the London Music Shop in Great Portland Street, Chimes in Marylebone High Street, and Foyles in the Charing Cross Road. The last in particular was an Aladdin's cave. Much of the stock had lain there since before the war, it seemed, and you never knew what you might find. When you did find it, still pre-war priced, you'd take it to an assistant, who would write out a bill which you took off to the cashier. Then you took your stamped bill back to the assistant, and hoped no-one had walked off with your parcel. All very different now, of course, though there are lovely surprises. My old friend Eric Forder, who still puts in an occasional appearance at Schott's, ordered some Poulenc songs for me from Salabert's warehouse in Paris. They were not Poulenc's most popular songs, and they arrived in the pristine first printing from 1942. French music seems at all times to have been printed on reject toilet paper – it rots and tears and eventually just decomposes before your eyes – I have reams of Chaminade and Turina that can barely stay upright on the stand – and in 1942 that was even more the case. But with these Poulenc prints that hadn't seen the light of day for seventy years, for once you could see the original beauty of the stuff.

Classical music was a bit stuffy when I was a child. Not deliberately, but perhaps the people that ran it were a bit stuffy themselves. After the Second World War, I think, everyone wanted to resume the concert manners of the thirties, and that set things back a while. So I welcome the new approach, to make classical music as accessible as possible. Even when the efforts seem a bit desperate, it's better than ignoring people and hoping you can just get on with doing your thing. Academia is making similar efforts, with its new buzzword of Impact.

I've probably already made it abundantly clear that I welcome the new tolerance of comprehensibility in composition. Another wonderful thing is the excellence of new concert halls. I have mixed opinions on the huge expansion of all aspects of arts management, but the days are over when just one person could run the whole business of the Turner Sims Concert Hall – the musical world it has to cover is just too big now.

BN: And I think the role of the venue is broader, all arts organisations are more conscious than they once were of their social role, their social utility, too.

Who are the people who've lit up the form for you, the interesting people? You've worked with a lot of great musicians, and I imagine a lot of them spring to mind – but perhaps there are others whose work has held your attention from a distance, too?

DON: Living musicians I admire whom I've never met....
Vengerov the violinist, Dudamel the conductor, Zimerman the
pianist, Brautigam the fortepianist (and pianist), Branford
Marsalis the saxophonist, Corigliano the composer. Would very
much like to have met George Martin and Arthur Rubinstein.
I'm glad I knew Sir John Drummond, a real visionary. A great
influence on me, though an all too brief one, was Peter Wishart.
With my piano teacher, Alex Kelly, and Brian Trowell, he
apparently made up a terrible triumvirate of brilliant and somewhat disruptive students on the London music scene back in the
50s. I met him when he was Professor at Reading University,
and there was some scheme to get young performers into
universities. It didn't come off, and I sometimes wonder how my
life would have developed if I'd moved into the university sector
twenty years earlier than I actually did. I dare say I'd have
missed a lot of fascinating experiences. But Wishart continued
a kindly interest in my career, and in particular, I imbibed his
wonderful book on harmony, which people still don't
understand, sixty years after he wrote it. That book brackets him
with another man who influenced me from a distance, David
Wulstan. He was one of the more flamboyant lecturers in my
time at Oxford, and somehow we kept in touch over the years.
He asked me to comment on the draft of his last book, *Listen
Again*, which took up the harmonic cudgels where Wishart had
left them, and I felt very flattered when he asked me to provide
his Preface. Marvellous books, and marvellous minds, though
few people know their work.

BN: What was music for, when you started playing, who used it,
and how did they use it? Has that changed since you started? I

wonder whether the role of festivals in making music available to people has led to meaningful change in the way it's used, or the people who use it.

DON: No-one 'used' music when I started! It would have seemed a most incongruous word. I half think it must have come in with sponsorship, though that's been around longer than we think: Beecham's Pills used to publish a monthly musical magazine. There was a lot of talk about 'using' when Benson & Hedges sponsored the Gold Award for Singers at Aldeburgh. This was generally thought to be a cynical thing, even though Dietrich Fischer-Dieskau was a forty-a-day man in those days. I was the official accompanist, and the organisers used to give us, and the competitors, strict instructions on the party line.

That use of the word 'using' still implies disapproval, doesn't it? 'Using', simply in the sense of consuming, perhaps belongs to the period when 'passengers' became 'customers' – when we all became consumers, in fact. The idea of a selected, carefully constructed lifestyle has something to do with it. Television advertising must have helped. There's always been advertising, but the mantra that 'hands that do dishes can be soft as your face', and the fact that 'Murray mints, Murray mints' were the 'too good to hurry mints', are indelibly, and reinforcingly, associated in my mind with musical jingles and pictures.

So a more fractured society, instead of following precedent, and enjoying the music it found around it, perhaps started to be choosey, especially as more and more sorts of music clamoured for attention. You can see it happening in the reminiscences of post-war jazz fans, who became zealous converts to their particular sort of music, and now often find themselves left behind by the tide, or so they lament. Technology helped too: it's easier to 'use' a Walkman than a wind-up gramophone. None of this is bad, of course, but it's good to realize how certain changes came about.

Festivals – classical music festivals – are mainly a post-war phenomenon: Edinburgh and Aldeburgh were the first. They were different from the long-established, mainly choral festivals in Norwich, Birmingham, Leeds, and so on, taking advantage of a new mobility both of audience and artist. The hundreds of festivals that sprang up were a way of harnessing local support, and spreading central funding, for what can be too predominantly metropolitan an art form, and a way of bringing fashionable culture to a fashion-conscious audience that lived out the mainly English (partly British) dream of living in the country – you still see that juncture particularly clearly with Country-House opera. There are specialist festivals that focus on contemporary music or chamber music or English music or art-song, and these do a very useful job. Other, more general, festivals are much more varied than they used to be, and you're as likely to see a fire-eater as a fiddler. Festivals have enriched the musical world. I'm not sure they changed *how* people listen, but they've certainly expanded *what* they listen to.

The rise of festivals has been paralleled by a slight decline in music clubs, at least as places of fashionable resort. A festival draws people in who would never dream of 'belonging' to an organisation that meets regularly once a month to hear a concert that the committee has chosen. All the music clubs I know are experimenting with new ways of reaching out, but it's difficult. A common lament, voiced by the members themselves, is that everyone's too old. I try not to worry too much about that.

Everyone's been 'too old' for several generations now – there's a never-ending supply of old people. Whenever this sort of conversation comes up, I recall a debate on music broadcasting that I arranged when I was Gresham Professor. The famously outspoken Natalie Wheen read out, in contemptuous tones, an official description of the average Radio 3 listener: 'White, male, late-middle-aged, and living in the south-east of England'. Whereupon, just such a man, sitting in the front row, snapped: 'What are you going to do about that, then? Shoot us all?'

BN: Do you think there are ways the trade has succeeded or failed in the way it's developed? I don't think this sort of thing happens ever so often – most of art is just putting on a show in a building, then using the box office to pay the rent, and the larger trends take a long time to play out. But do you see triumphs and disasters that have played out over the past fifty years?

DON: The Proms have improved. Opera has survived and flourished. Orchestras are reaching out – that's all those new concert management jobs. The changes in the hard-pressed record industry are not all bad. One of the strange things about the classical music world immediately after WWII is how it was dominated by a few people who found themselves in a favourable position to move immediately into the musical vacuum. They were often great artists, but perhaps they weren't the only great artists, just the lucky ones. Their dominance was sealed by contracts with the big record companies. It's much easier now to be a recorded musician, and that's a good thing.

The array of musicians that can occupy the public's mind is

somewhat expanded, too. In the 60s and 70s there was a remarkable group of piano competition winners, mainly living in London, who dominated most people's ideas of the future of the piano: Radu Lupu, Stephen Kovacevich, Murray Peraiha, Alfred Brendel and so on. I met a lot of these artists when I made a programme about André Tchaikovsky, a complete maverick of a pianist and composer, now best known for having left his skull to the RSC for use in *Hamlet*. (The interview with his agent about how he had to boil the head was grisly in the extreme.) All these great musicians had the utmost respect for their little-known colleague – just to take one example, the violinist Peter Cropper described playing through the Brahms Piano Quintet with him, and how Tchaikovsky put up the copy but never bothered to turn the first page, playing the whole thing from memory. Kovacevich said that when Lupu gave the first performance of André Tchaikovsky's Piano Concerto in the Royal Festival Hall, if a bomb had fallen on it, that would have been the end of all the pianists in London. I think there would be more room for such a musician these days, more notice taken – though perhaps not for very long.

In Montreal this spring, I was thrilled to meet Richard Bruno, 'the father of the CD'. He worked for Philips, and the majority of CD-related patents are in his name. The CD must be the most significant thing in classical music during the last fifty years. It stimulated a great re-recording of all the familiar repertoire, and it gave a huge boost to 'early music', which had just reached the necessary critical mass to be able to take advantage of it. It's hard to come to terms with its eventual demise, as the world moves to download only. The content and order of an album in any recorded medium has always been a matter of great care. It's dismaying to think that the downloader can negate all that without even reading the notes that would explain things. That's both a symptom and a cause of not just a shortening, but a narrowing, of attention. More and more people listen to fewer and fewer pieces, and the occasional widenings of the popular repertoire (do you remember Gorecki?) seem both fortuitous and short-lived. But as I've said, festivals can go some way to balancing this, and so too can universities, which in the last twenty years have vastly expanded their role as promoters (and guardians) of a wide and intelligently assessed repertoire of music in performance.

The most debilitating thing about contemporary musical culture is the reprehensible use of the word 'song' to describe any piece of music: but here I start to sound like Basil Fawlty. 'Racket? That's Brahms! Brahms' Third Racket!'

Writing

BN: We arrive now at the final movement of our book. Having explored the world you came from, and the world you moved through, I propose to examine the products of those hinterlands – the things you've had to say.

I wanted to do this partly because when you and I were touring our collaboration *HengeMusic* in 2015 – of which more later – I had a distinct sense of a cycle of work coming to completion for you, that I thought ought to be acknowledged and given some attention. The reasons for that work's importance, I hope I've outlined in the preceding movements of this book.

I should also say that the other reason I wanted to make this book, that I hope we've been exploring allusively, is that I think this route we're taking through your life is the route we all take into knowing the world. Coming from one set of circumstances, and finding our way through the mutability of the times we live in, and finally formulating a sense of ourselves, that all of us express in one way or another, and a few choose to express through writing, or writing music, seems to me to be a universal route through life that richly rewards close attention. So this book is as much an attempt to explore the way everyone comes to see things the way they do, and believe what they believe, as it is an attempt to assess your work. It's just much easier when you explore it through the life of an artist, because they publish the outcomes of all this living, and give them titles, and provide something solid you can analyse!

I think the compositions you produced between 2013 and

2015 – your completed Piano Concerto in C and Symphony; *Sterne, was The Man; Turning Points* and *Henge Music* – were the third coherent cycle of work you've produced to date. The first was the activity of your Academy years; the second was a rediscovery of the act of composition in the Noughties that saw you produce the song cycles *Think Only This* and *Tomorrow nor Yesterday* and the oratorio *Prayerbook*, as well as the initial version of your Piano Concerto, between 2001 and 2008. As we'll see, these quite focused windows of productivity in no way reflect the time spent writing the pieces, which develop over quite different timescales, but it's interesting to see how the first performances cluster. It seems to me that the third, more recent cycle of projects began in earnest with the Symphony, and also with your decision to revise the Piano Concerto.

First, I'm interested in the revisions you undertook of the Piano Concerto. That decision to revisit something, which we'll address later, always strikes me as indicative of some development in who you are and what you have to say? I think you also revised *Tomorrow nor Yesterday* at this time as well.

DON: The first version of the Piano Concerto was written for a very small band, for economic reasons. But the material was really conceived for something with a bit more oomph, so when I got the chance to put on a concert with a large orchestra, I added extra instruments to the Concerto. My techniques had changed since I first wrote the piece, especially through the rhythmic procedures I'd found through writing my Symphony, so I improved the Concerto material in some of its rhythmic details, and expanded the ending. That's the version we recorded. I wouldn't want the earlier version ever to be performed now.

As to the song-cycle, it lacked contrast in the middle, so for a 60th birthday concert I added an extra song. That song also played with rhythm in a new way, but since I wrote it while I was composing the Symphony, it actually contributed to the techniques I was working on.

BN: As I understand it, the early compositions that date from your Academy years, and the occasional compositions you made during the 90s for festival occasions, are all withdrawn. You've already mentioned that you felt you didn't cohere your artistic identity until the time you started at Southampton and recorded your discs of the World's First Piano Concertos and Elgar's Complete Piano Music, so I imagine you feel that all those earlier compositions are preparatory, exploratory statements.

DON: That's right. I was exploring a great deal, but not discovering any Lost Cities.

BN: Are you interested in spending some time on your comic operas, where do they fit in? As well as *Die! Sober Flirter*, you wrote a piece called *The Jolly Roger*, about ten years ago now. Interestingly, neither of them fall within those two main periods of activity that I've mentioned. Notwithstanding the wit and playfulness that's evident throughout your work and very much evident in these two pieces, they seem to sit slightly apart from the rest, for me. Is that unfair?

DON: I'm very grateful to *Die! Sober Flirter*. As I explained earlier, the plot prescribed very simply the language that I had to use – Mozart-plus. There were two good things about that. First, no-one knew what Mozart-plus might have been, so I still had some creative work to do in establishing the language. But, however I established it, it would be more or less immune from criticism, and so I could concentrate on what I needed to say. I found that an incredibly liberating experience, absolutely analogous to how I felt, stepping onto a stage after I'd had my row with Mme. Lefebure. *The Jolly Roger* was, amongst other things, a tribute to my friend David Pocock, the dedicatee of *Die! Sober Flirter* – I first met him just as I was completing that. Like *Die!*, *Roger* is for just three voices, and also like *Die!* it plays with the radio medium by presenting things that can't easily be staged. *Roger* goes much further, though – the Cabin Boy sings a waltz song, while bound, gagged, and walking the plank. David Pocock, who I was very upset to learn passed away while we were working on this book, was a brilliant raconteur and a great teller of jokes. One of his best was the Pirate joke, and a plot occurred to me, loosely based on the characters of Captain Pugwash, that depended upon the Pirate joke for its explanation. Consequently, I made a set-piece scene of party pieces in the middle of the opera, where the tenor sang a duet with himself, to tell the Pirate joke. Not all the music is quintessentially me, but I suspect that may not be a bad thing on the musical stage. Peripheral though it may be to what I think of as my composing path, I drew useful lessons from *The Jolly Roger* when I came to write *STERNE, was THE MAN*, and I propose to draw many more when I finally get round to my next operatic project, *The Body in the Ballroom*, which I think will *all* be me.

BN: They certainly played a role, then.

Now, what I hope we've been preparing all this while is a framework that listeners might be able to use when approaching your work. It's my contention that exploring the cultural hinterland to the compositions you've produced enriches the way those pieces speak – as I began by saying, in order to begin to understand someone, you have to understand where they came from, the place where the river rises. So a large part of the apparatus for listening to your work that I hoped to put in place is already behind us – it's the stories we've been telling up till now. But the last thing I intend to do is look specifically at the pieces I hope people will listen to with a new perspective having read this book, and try to draw out a few details about them. I must stress that I myself am no musicologist – I am opening up conversations here, I'm by no means the best person to take them through to their conclusion. What I hope is that others will follow after this work, and seek to detail some of the ideas we've tried to examine. But in the mean time, I just want to look at the work and hear a little of what you have to say about it.

*

Think only this was first performed on 21st March 2002 at Lancaster University by Philip Langridge (tenor), Jennifer Langridge (cello) and the composer (piano).

It has been recorded by the same artists on Prelude Records (released 2010), and by Mark Wilde, Joseph Spooner and the composer on EM Records (released 2013).

*

BN: You've already introduced us to the initiating impulse that started *Think only this*, the cycle of settings of Great War poetry that I think marks the beginning of your mature work as a composer. And you've said it felt natural to work in the language of the poetry you were setting, and then to do what Britten does with *Winter Words*, say, and complicate what you do through the accompaniment. I have an impression that this cycle came quite naturally, that you wrote it quite quickly – did you tell me once that the opening melody came fully formed to you while you were pottering round the house?

DON: Not so much pottering round – as soon as I opened the book. The score tells me that I wrote it between September 2001 and March 2002, so not very swiftly really, I suppose.

BN: Were the settings the first ideas that came to mind, were there discarded options? Did you pore over books before selecting the poems, or were they favourites?

DON: Three were favourites – *In Flanders Fields*, *Base Details*, and *The Soldier*. I needed something more narrative for contrast, and found Sassoon's *Counter-Attack*. *Base Details* was about all I knew of Sassoon till then. I cherish a letter from his literary executor, telling me how much Sassoon would have enjoyed the music.

BN: You've said that the instrumentation suggested itself because you were working with Philip and Jennifer Langridge when the idea came to you – a singer and a cellist. Does that imply that you were writing quite practically, for performance, from the start? Did you think about suiting Philip's voice? Did you mention it to them before the work was written? Or was it just that you were inspired by what was to hand, and the idea of performance wasn't as closely connected?

DON: It was very definitely intended for insertion into the programme we were performing, and I had Philip's voice in mind all the time I was writing it – though I've been delighted to hear it from other tenors too. I didn't mention it until it was finished – it was a rather delicate matter. Philip had a great reverence for composers, and he thought of me in a very different way, as his performing colleague. I felt that for me suddenly to tear off my false moustaches, as it were, might change the nature of our relationship: he might not be prepared to accept me as a composer, he might think I was trying to take advantage of him. When I eventually broached the subject with him, he was immensely surprised, but he loved the piece, and so did Jennifer, so all was well.

BN: As a rule, do you make a habit of discussing work with people before it's completed, or is that something you avoid?

DON: I don't discuss my compositions as I make them. It seems a rather less collaborative and much more purely personal procedure than making a radio or television programme. As you've pointed out, I do sometimes revise them!

BN: You've said the piece came about out of the juxtaposition of performing Great War music on 9/11. Knowing that slightly deepens the way the cycle works on me, I must say. On the surface, it's a quite consciously, sophisticatedly beautiful meditation on the sorrows of that conflict, phrasing the Great War as a tragedy, arguably perpetrated by the ruling classes on those who suffered. (I'm thinking of the sardonic setting of 'Base Details'.) It communicates in the musical language of the period, but as you listen to the work, I think there is a sense that that language is somewhat refracted by the lines the accompanying instruments take beneath the voice – it's a little like listening to Edwardian music through glass.

DON: That's a pleasing thought. It reminds me of what Sarah Baldock, the organist who toured our *HengeMusic* said, when she first heard my Symphony. The recapitulation of the slow movement's main theme, in D flat instead of the original D, made her think of a sepia photograph of the original coloured scene.

BN: In the context of its initiating impulse, 9/11, that voice you chose for the work is a little more complex, and interesting, I think. I suppose what's rewarding to reconcile is that elegiac and beautiful tone in the work, and the absolute brutality of the images of the Twin Towers that must have been around you while you wrote. Of course, people sought out beauty in those as well – I'm thinking of the 'Falling Man' photo – and the First World War was a parade of atrocities and horrors that numbed most of those who witnessed them to the point of permanent silence, so the elegiac and the horrific co-exist in both events, but the choice to respond to that initiating impulse by remembering past atrocities through the wistful lens of this work is interesting.

DON: It's the beginning and the end (which recapitulates the first tune) that's wistful. The parody of *It's a long way to Tipperary* (*Base Details*) gets angry, but you're right, that's all contained within the wistful impulse. Brooke was seeking beauty in *The*

Soldier. You could say that's because he never really found out what the war was like, dying of a mosquito bite on the way. But perhaps that also means that his particular view of the whys and wherefores of the War remained clear – the same view that so many had at first. By placing that poem at the end of my cycle, I give it a certain ironic weight. And the self-indulgent beauty of its music adds a different weight to it, something that goes beyond mere pathos, I hope, and beyond mere tragedy. Some people might not think that wistfulness could trump tragedy, but you can't really analyse the effect without sitting and listening to it.

BN: When I started writing my second novel, which for various reasons was a very difficult and personal book for me to write, I clung to a song by the singer Sun Kil Moon called 'Carissa'. The first chorus runs: 'Carissa was thirty-five/ You don't just raise two kids and take out the trash and die./ She was my second cousin/ I didn't know her well at all, but that doesn't mean that I wasn't/ Meant to find some poetry/ To make some sense of this, to find a deeper meaning/ In this senseless tragedy, O Carissa I'll sing your name across every sea.' What he expresses, very profoundly I think, is the role art plays in reclaiming the tragedies that befall us and allowing us to find space for the terrible in our lives, rather than shut it off and hide it away in the subconscious, where it can only do psychic damage. Thinking about *Think Only This* has brought that idea to mind for me quite strongly.

DON: That song puts it well. And what about Wilfred Owen? He brings tragedy, art and a healing compassion even closer. '...War and the pity of War. The Poetry is in the pity'.

BN: How did the cycle's first performance come about?

DON: It was put straight into the next Great War concert we had in the diary – we were travelling that programme about a lot at the time.

*

Tomorrow nor Yesterday (revised version) was first publicly performed on 19th January 2013 at the Cathedral School, Lincoln by Mark Wilde (tenor) & the composer (piano). The same artists recorded it March 31st – April 2nd 2013, in the Turner Sims Concert Hall, University of Southampton. (EMR CD015). The cycle sets the following poems by John Donne.

1.   The Flea

2.   The Sunne Rising

3.   Aire and Angels

4.   The Baite

5.   The Expiration

6.   The good-morrow

7.   The Anniversarie

*

BN: Donne has always been important to you, hasn't he. And indeed, you've been setting him for a long time – *Tomorrow nor Yesterday* includes a song set long ago.

DON: I wrote *The Expiration* at Oxford, in 1974. I couldn't quite make it do what I wanted, back then – it was great to return to it after thirty years or so and find when I revised it that my technique had improved. Some of the melodic shapes for *The good-morrow* are even earlier. I tried to set that poem almost as soon as my brother gave me the Grierson edition as my 1968 Christmas present, but I hadn't got the harmonic language to make the shapes work. Once I'd got the harmonies right, I had to simplify the shape quite drastically: I'd been trying to make the melodic line do everything on its own.

BN: What is it that matters to you in Donne?

DON: The fact that I'm never quite sure what he means! Even when I think at least that I've got to the bottom layer of all his possible meanings.

BN: Where did the idea of the cycle come from? Was Britten a conscious factor? I know the first recording of *Tomorrow nor Yesterday* was released along with *The Holy Sonnets of John Donne*.

DON: Britten was a factor in a curious way, as you'll see. Once I'd found a voice in *Think only this* I had to decide how best to develop it. Stanford, the great composition teacher, always made his students write songs for their first year or so – I often think it was that single pedagogical quirk that created the colossal repertoire of twentieth-century English song. If he'd made everyone write a piano piece, English music would look very different: that's what Percy Sherwood would have done, I suppose. Perhaps Stanford found that the fairly prescribed emotional message of the sort of verse his students chose to set, enabled him to concentrate his comments on technical processes – because that's what he did, as far as the songs go that I've seen – some of the songs I recorded by Muriel Herbert, Claire Tomalin's mother, are covered in Stanford's pencil. If it had been a piano piece, Stanford would have had to start by discussing the material as well as the spacing of the chords or the doubled leading-notes. In a song he could just make sure the scansion was correct, and move on.

Anyway, when I started to revise my ancient Donne songs, I found that, apart from anything else, they were ideal vehicles to study a particular technical problem. Making myself a posthumous Stanford pupil was on the whole quite helpful, and I carried on till I'd got a cycle-full.

BN: And were you writing for practical performance once again? I think Mark Wilde premiered both the original and revised versions of the piece – he's someone you began working with perhaps fifteen years ago, and have done a great deal with since. Was he someone you were writing for specifically?

DON: Yes, I had him very much in mind when I was writing them. The first song in particular, *The Flea*, depends on his brilliant comic opera-bility. He needs to conjure up the young Donne, setting out his cunning arguments, but somehow the silent woman needs to be there too, triumphantly winning the argument by killing the flea. I composed a sharp intake of breath for that moment, and that's a device Mark's made his own. In this first song of the cycle, the voice starts before the piano, and that's a trick he brings off effortlessly too. I suppose it's been done before, but as you know, I don't worry too much about that. Finally, the fact that his first word is 'Mark' – 'Mark but this flea' – is my private joke.

BN: You talked about Donne's intellectualism in the liner notes to this cycle when it was recorded. What strikes me, though, is that you've actually gathered together a palette of poems that is more closely preoccupied with the romantic and metaphysical than, say, the theological, of which there's plenty in Donne. This is a point worth extending slightly – we'll see as we go forwards through your work that actually you're quite happy to set whatever's useful to you, appendices to prayerbooks, gravestone epitaphs, hashtags, etc. You're not someone who lives within the constraints of any idea of 'appropriate' or 'inaproppriate' source material, you work in found poetry, as we've raised earlier in the context of your university office's photocopier. So the choice of material here, while on the surface quite a conventional one, is perhaps interesting in the context of your wider work. Does the piece have a metaphysical argument? Or a romantic element? At this stage, had the more eclectic way of gathering material that I'd say characterises your recent work occurred to you, or did poems still seem like the natural thing to set to music?

DON: This is where Britten comes in. I think his *Holy Sonnets* are by far his best set of songs. Other composers have tried setting the sacred side of Donne too. Fewer have tried the profane side. Steering away from the much-musicked Holy Sonnets meant my songs could fill a comparative vacuum – I mentioned that the lack of liturgical music in my output has a similar cause. It was clear in my mind that it would be better to complement Britten than to compete, and also that the best way of getting these songs out in the world would be via a recording rather than a publication. And so the idea of a cycle that would sit alongside the Britten entered my mind early on. I selected poems that had aspects I particularly liked – the impetuous rhythm of *Busie old fool*, the dispassionate, self-sufficient disdain of *Aire and Angels* (if indeed it means what I thought it meant) – and added them to the more conventional poems I had attempted long before.

BN: You also make an interesting observation about Donne's translation of the emotions into an intellectual language being quite an interesting study for musicians.

DON: Yes, musicians have to intellectualise their emotions too: they have to be filtered through numerous techniques, from the visceral impact of melody & harmony, past hard-won instrumental skills, and on to the deeper intellectual mysteries of counterpoint and the fine balance of form. So 'At the round earth's imagin'd corners' is musical even before we get to the trumpeting angels. The intellectual tangle of simultaneously admitting, yet proposing to ignore, a knowledge of the earth's true shape, produces, not a mess, but a poetic image all the more potent for its artificiality. It's like some great proposition of Bach, the violin Chaconne, say, where a constructed harmonic shape is mysteriously endowed with emotional power precisely because of its artificiality.

BN: I think John Carey's observation that Donne's work creates a 'provokingly questionable' and unstable relationship between writing and experience was in your mind as well, you wanted to explore that interplay and its complexities.

DON: The relationship between writing and experience becomes very real when you consider the boundaries between song and opera. When I was running those song masterclasses in Chicago, we had a great row one year about Vaughan Williams's song *The Roadside Fire*. 'I will make you brooches', it begins, and it's addressed to some beloved object of Robert Louis Stevenson's. Our European singers that year accepted that as the song's context, and simply got on with singing it unaffectedly to the audience, to the great satisfaction of the European tutors on the course. But that Chicago audience much preferred the performance of an American singer, who made it into a scene from an opera, striding round the stage, warming his hands at the roadside fire, cajoling the beloved with gestures of hands and arms, even stepping over the stream at one point. The same abyss beckons with any song that includes the pronoun 'I'. (I can't help noticing that hundreds of modern worship songs begin with 'I', while about the most personal the old hymnbooks got was the single hymn 'When I survey the wondrous cross'. Modern worship songs are basically in an American style, and it may be the same social attitudes at work in Graham Kendrick and in this particular performance of Vaughan Williams.)

Carey's point is that 'when Donne writes 'So, so, break off this last lamenting kiss', no one believes he wrote the poem when breaking off a kiss, and whether there was a kiss at all seems debatable'. The court-room logic of *The Flea*, the tortuous spiritual anatomy of *The Anniversarie*, all require the singer to walk a tightrope of abstraction across the abyss of representation. I love that sort of risky precision performance. It's a bit like playing very difficult piano music – do you let on, do you demonstrate the difficulty to your audience, or do you sail imperturbably through it all?

BN: For all that *Think only this* is rendered soulful by its subject matter, I think that tonally, *Tomorrow nor Yesterday* is a much more haunted and indeed wistful piece. There's a movement away from the deliciousness of melodic narrative as well, a subtle complicating and undermining of the beautiful surface of the poetry you're setting, that again for me suggests a relationship with Britten – primarily with *Winter Words*, which you've spoken admiringly of already. That cycle is full of underminings that remind me of *Tomorrow nor Yesterday*. The search, you've said, was for 'that fugitive ambiguity so prized in music, where each listener hears a different meaning'.

DON: I was being quite serious when I said I liked the fact that I don't quite know what Donne means! Thanks to the abstract nature of musical language itself, only very simple music has a stable relationship to experience. The composer needs to allow his audience the same freedom that he allows his performers.

BN: From what you've already said about your decision to revise the work, I gather you weren't entirely satisfied with it, at least at first. Perhaps that was resolved by your revisions? It seems to me as successful now as anything you've made, in its delicately poised and quite cautious, coy relationship with its material, and with its listener.

DON: I'm glad to hear that. And I like the word you use, 'made'. As we've been discussing, the whole thing needs to be artificial, unreal; and the addition of *The Baite*, exploring the rhythmic language I was working on for my Symphony, was a necessary lightening. You have to be careful not to overfreight your pinnace, to borrow a phrase from the third song!

BN: In the decade since you first took up writing *Tomorrow nor Yesterday*, you haven't come back to the song cycle as a form. There have been many performances of these two cycles, but to date you haven't started a new project in the same vein. This seems to me to be in part a result of increasing resources for performance, allowing you to work more ambitiously, and increasing technical ambition in what you do. You have revisited the idea of music and poems in *HengeMusic*, which we'll address in a little while; but I wondered whether the song cycle form in its clearest sense, as practised here, is something that has lost its attraction you? Or are you just waiting for the idea you can work with?

DON: It's Time's wingèd chariot again, I'm afraid. I could write something much more interesting in the time I was writing another song. And Professor Stanford has moved me on to the next thing.

BN: Perhaps it's worth asking, at this point, how conscious you actually are about the particular forms you write in. Do the pieces just suggest themselves, and happen organically, or are there particular peaks you look to scale, or artists or instruments you're eager to work with that organise what you do?

DON: I don't think I'd ever pick an artist and then think, what can I write?, though once I've decided to write something, I'm likely to have someone in mind – Peter Savidge for *Prayerbook*, John Harle for *HengeMusic*. I'm very conscious of genre, especially when I find myself working out a new one. So probably my music has two faces: one when I'm consciously writing a Piano Concerto to join all the other piano concertos, or a Symphony to join the other symphonies; and another when I'm working out how to set a sermon to music, or how to give form to 400 years of theological argument, or how to set Cluedo to music.

*

Prayerbook: an oratorio about Tradition & Change, was first performed on 23rd October 2006 in Dorchester Abbey by the Oxford Bach Choir conducted by Nicholas Cleobury, with Peter Savidge (baritone) and the composer (organ), as part of the English Music Festival.

It was recorded on 13th & 14th September 2012 in Romsey Abbey by the Waynflete Singers conducted by the composer, with Peter Savidge (baritone) and David Coram (organ). (EMRCD 0010)

Part One – Faith
1.   Prelude – God the Father
2.   Preface
3.   Aria : On Miracles
4.   The Litany
5.   Hymn : O God, our help in ages past

*

BN: There are two epigraphs to this piece:

'Tradition is not a noun shaped once and for all in the past; it is a verb active under God now for the sake of the future.' David E. Jenkins Bishop of Durham: 6th July 1986, York

And:

'Change is the nursery
Of music, joy, life and eternity.'
                    John Donne

Can you talk about those?

DON: As the subtitle makes clear, the piece is all about the relationship between Tradition and Change – we've discussed those things earlier in our book. We've discussed Donne too – you can imagine how I'd quote him in support of an idea. Then, I'm a great admirer of David Jenkins. I wrote to him after hearing him speak on the radio, and we corresponded from time to time. As it happens, he was a pupil of Warden Nineham, so I felt I knew slightly where his ideas were coming from, which may have helped me understand them – that's the premise of this book, after all. I felt his ideas were absolutely necessary, and very clearly the present outcome of the whole Anglican journey. And because *Prayerbook* is a sincere piece, and a piece about contemporary ideas of faith, I needed to include those ideas in the piece. I chose the epigraph partly because it looks to the future through a development of tradition, just as I try to; and partly because of its fruitful genre-bending confusion between the parts of speech, a technical device that appeals to me very much.

David's contributions to the libretto come from his book *God, miracle, and the Church of England*. I love this title for its disingenuous, deceptive bathos. I needed to change a word. The line 'I have become engaged in many arguments', when set repetitively to music, ends up as 'I have become engaged', which is not quite the same thing. So David allowed me to substitute the word 'involved'.

BN: How did *Prayerbook* come to be written?

DON: I conceived a good deal of the musical material for *Prayerbook* while driving, with the pragmatic filter that if I couldn't remember it by the time I got to my destination and was able to write it down, then it hadn't been strong enough for inclusion. The Canon on 'In heavenly love abiding' is a heavily revised version of a piece I wrote for my grandmother's funeral forty-odd years ago, the most striking change being that the two-part canon is played on two manuals by just one hand: the left hand, thus freed, is able to re-define the harmony on a third manual. I wrote the Double Fugue during a lengthy journey on New York's A-train during an April heatwave. The section that took longest to write was the Cadenza for the Organ Pedals, which required an allusive rather than an explicit harmonic language.

BN: It sounds like the process was partly about the coagulation of lots of sequences into a larger whole. That makes me wonder whether the piece something you found yourself doing incrementally, or whether there was a grander vision you were shaping your writing towards. What made you want to set the Prayer Book in the first place?

DON: The Prayerbook has come to mean a fixed and archaic thing in the Church of England. Its Prefaces over the years tell a different story. In 1549 it said:

'There was never any thing by the wit of man so well devised, or so sure established, which in continuance of time hath not been corrupted.'

And:

'In this our time, the minds of men are so diverse; some think it a great matter of conscience to depart from a piece of the least of their ceremonies, they be so addicted to their old customs; and again on the other side, some be so new-fangled, that they would innovate all things, and so despise the old, that nothing can like them, but that it is new.'

To which the 1662 Preface added, with just a hint of Restoration smugness:

'It hath been the wisdom of the Church of England to keep the mean between the two extremes.'

This is magnificent writing, for a start, and then it's so contemporary, so very Now – and has been at every moment since 1549. John Keble took up the cudgels in the 1820s, attempting to correct a perceived lurch toward the new:

'It is the peculiar happiness of the Church of England to possess, in her authorized formularies, an ample provision for both a sound rule of faith and a sober standard of feeling. But in times of much leisure and unbounded curiosity, when excitement of every kind is sought after with a morbid eagerness, this part of the merit of our liturgy is likely to be lost: the very tempers, which most require such discipline, setting themselves most decidedly against it. The charge might perhaps surprise them, just as, in other times and countries, the impatient patrons of innovation are surprised at finding themselves rebuked on religious grounds.'

Such fervent moderation, so radically expressed, is fascinating, and it seemed to me that it was time to reveal the struggle that everyone seemed to have forgotten in the Prayerbook. Of course, as they wearily concluded in 1662:

'We know it impossible to please all; nor can expect that men of factious, peevish, and perverse spirits should be satisfied with any thing that can be done in this kind by any other than themselves.'

BN: You've spoken convincingly about the book's cultural importance.

DON: It was written by unsuspected poets, and its glorious cadences were familiar for four hundred years. The language couldn't ignore it. Even today, you can learn a thing or two from where Cranmer put a semi-colon and where a colon.

BN: How did you hope to amplify or explore that through your music?

DON: I used various musical devices to illuminate the meaning of the text. The starkness of the Litany calls forth a brutal march; the Table of Kindred (a list of rules) is a classic double-fugue; the eschatology of A Dark Speaking is expressed in an obsessive Chaconne. The three instrumental pieces representing the Persons of God are combined to symbolize the Trinity. The Father is represented by Harmony, the Son by the human impulse of Melody, slightly hallowed as an organ fugue, while the Holy Ghost is mainly Rhythm.

BN: To your knowledge, had anyone actually set this material before? It's quite something if no one else had got round to it – in a culture as musical as the one the Prayer Book springs from. That takes me back to my idea about the dramatic breaching of convention that this, and other recent pieces represent, when you take a good look at them. You start breaking through to this idea of found poetry here, by setting something people normally think of as sitting *next* to the book with the songs in.

DON: I don't think anyone else has set the Prefaces. Probably Tyndale's not set much either – and although there are other settings of the Litany, I doubt if they try to place it in an ironically macabre context, which seems to me to be a way of sympathetically entering the medieval mind. I love reading Prefaces: you find out all sorts of things. Vaughan Williams's preface to the *English Hymnal*, for instance, floats the idea of melody as morality, which is an excellent counterpart to James Lyon's 'tune as myth'.

BN: At the time you wrote it, this was by far the biggest piece you'd undertaken. Not necessarily a vast undertaking in terms of instrumentation, of course, but a lot of bodies in space, and the ambition of the material seems really striking. Did that commission seek you out, or did you want to make a larger work, or was this more incidental to what you were doing? And had you been thinking about working towards this when you were writing the song cycles?

DON: Setting the Prayerbook prefaces had been in my mind for a long time. The complicated part was working out how to give the piece a shape. I seized on the charm of threes – Faith, Hope, Charity; Father, Son, Holy Ghost; Harmony, Melody, Rhythm;

Old Testament, New Testament, Revelation. I think it was this shape that appealed to Em Marshall-Luck, the founder-director of the English Music Festival, when I suggested it to her.

BN: And the piece was premiered at the English Music Festival, which has played an important role in supporting you and getting your work heard over the last decade. I think the same could be said for a great many composers, along with its associated label, EM Records.

DON: They've done an enormous amount of really important work.

BN: How long did the piece take to write? Was it difficult?

DON: The main difficulties of form were overcome once I'd compiled the libretto, and then I could simply create the flavours of the music. From the point of view of developing my musical language, the shortish movements were ideal. I knew that I needed to be able to combine my emblematic harmony, melody and rhythm, to make the piece that symbolises the Trinity, and I knew that I needed a formal double-fugue that would combine with all that material as well. That, combined with the strength of the libretto, gave me the imaginative space to enjoy myself. What I dream of is a partly staged performance, where the choral scholar quartet, appropriately robed, dance aggressively towards the chorus in the Litany, taunting them with ever more unpleasant fates, with the ladies of the chorus continually exclaiming 'Good Lord!'

I can't remember how long it took to write, but I do know that once again I revised it after a couple of performances.

There are three congregational hymns, two of which are elaborately arranged: O God, our help in ages past, and Personent hodie. 'O God' puts the congregation in canon with the chorus, which is a new thing, I think: congregations seem to rise to the challenge! Personent hodie is from Piae Cantiones, the mediaeval hymn book from Finland re-published by Thomas Helmore, the teacher of Arthur Sullivan – a book that I know very well, as a result of my interest in Sullivan's work. The reason for the song's inclusion, apart from its Epiphany theme, which fitted in at this point, was that the tune works contrapuntally with the Dies Irae, and my parallel theological plot also required the Last Trump, which is played by the three trombones, standing up. After these various devices, the third hymn, Love Divine, always seemed a bit tame – I had left it unadorned. So in the end, I composed my own tune, and since that rules out congregational participation, all sorts of things can happen in the last verse! I added a spectacular high trumpet part for that.

BN: And how did the process of rehearsal go? Presumably this was the most exposed you'd felt as a composer, the most musicians you'd had running the rule over your work.

DON: Rather as I felt about confessing to being a composer with Langridge and *Think only this*, I wasn't sure what Nicholas Cleobury would make of the oratorio, since he too knew me only as a performing colleague. I'm still not sure what Nick made of it, but I do know that the Oxford Bach Choir enjoyed it. I went up and played for the rehearsals in Jesus College Chapel, and we had our final rehearsal in Keble Chapel.

BN: The new element that comes in for me here as a listener, having spent time with the song cycles, is joy. Much of this piece strikes me as being absolutely joyous. There's a relish in the material, and also a delight in the instrumentations and the sheer noisiness of some of what's happening, the quirkier choices the piece takes in its instrumentation, the juxtaposition of text with musical styles. Of course the wit of all this is not new when we think about *Die! Sober Flirter*, but the wistfulness we found ourselves talking about in earlier pieces has taken a step back, I think a different energy drives this. Do you think that was the nature of your response to the material? Or your own life feeding in? Or just the pleasures of being able to play with more elements in the writing of a piece? It really has quite a strikingly ebullient, unvarnished energy, I think, particularly in the context of the festival which premiered it, which, in my experience, can produce some really quite civilised work, all quite neat and tucked in. This isn't neat. It's superbly anarchic to listen to, though the more you look at what you're doing, the more intricate and deliberately clever it becomes.

DON: I'd stopped worrying at this point whether people would 'approve' of my music. I'm delighted to think that you can tell that, just by hearing the joy. The other thing is that for choral music to come across properly, the chorus must enjoy singing it. I was very aware of that, and that probably affects the way it sounds.

BN: I suppose the other key factor here in the new tone you found is that you were writing for the organ. In your hands, I always find the organ becomes quite a cheeky, funny instrument – capable of immense creativity. And I have it in my mind that you've actually spent a lot of time over the years playing it as a way of arguing for its role in contemporary culture. Perhaps there's a cheerfulness to writing for an instrument you know so well?

DON: I've always been fascinated by organs. Teenage holidays in Devon turned into a game of Hunt the Organ Key that's still going on. Part of the appeal is that every instrument is different. A basic Open Diapason will carry each individual builder's notion of beauty, as well as his idea of how it fits into his scheme as a whole, and into the building's acoustic. So playing an organ becomes a question of adapting your ideas to fit the facts, which is a microcosm of life itself. Early pianos appeal to me for the same reason – the process of development and the luck of survival mean that they're all different too, by now.

Even when you're mainly playing just one organ, its potential mutability is always at the back of your mind. And so writing for organ becomes a search for the common ground in all organs – organs of a certain size, anyway. The way it actually turns out will be a mediation between what you want to happen, and what you think all organs can do. Every now and then, you can spice the compromises with a risk. I enjoy the process of twisting all these conditions to produce what I had in mind in the first place.

BN: And finally, you were writing for Dorchester Abbey. Had you played there before? How did that shape your ideas?

DON: I'd done a fortepiano concert in the Abbey for Music at Oxford. It's not a very cavernous place, but it does have just a hint of the lost-in-the-roof-space that I had in mind for the sound. The rehearsal in Keble the night before caught that well

– very exciting – and the recording in Romsey Abbey was exactly the right acoustic.

BN: I remember you going through the process of getting this piece performed absolutely charged with energy and, I think, confidence about it. And I think when you came out the other side, you were still noticeably charged with the same sense of conviction and purpose and confidence. Was it a piece and an experience that particularly satisfied you?

DON: It did. I wouldn't write it exactly the same now, so it's just as well that I wrote it then.

*

Piano Concerto in C was first performed on 27th May 2008 in Dorchester Abbey, directed from the piano by the composer, as part of the English Music Festival.
The revised version was first performed on 1st October 2015 in St. Paul's Church, Covent Garden, with the Orchestra of St. Paul's conducted by Ben Palmer, and the composer as soloist. This version was recorded on 8th January 2016 in Watford Town Hall by the BBC Concert Orchestra conducted by Gavin Sutherland, and the composer as soloist. (EMR CD037-8).

Allegro

Andante serioso

Allegro molto

*

BN: I think this is my favourite piece of yours. Its first performance, in its original, smaller orchestration, happened when I was nineteen or twenty, which is an impressionable age to hear something, and it's melodically very lovely, which is a delight at that age as well. I was listening to Rachmaninov a lot then, and was able to listen to this in a similar context. But the other reason it seems important to me as a piece is the time you've taken over it. Its first sketches predate me, I think!

DON: The first half of the main theme of the slow movement was written in Chicago in 1993: its second half is taken from *The Jolly Roger*. The first movement took its origin from a brief improvisation on the fanfare figure that opens *Sabbath Morning at Sea* in Elgar's *Sea Pictures*. That provided both the introduction and the second subject.

BN: Not quite older than me, then – but how striking to see how many threads it brings together. America, *The Jolly Roger*, Elgar. Was there other material you brought together here? You're making it sound quite like it's the product of technical exercises, but I always find it a very emotional piece. It's very different and perhaps difficult to discuss source material where there isn't a text the work is based on, isn't it.

DON: The second subject of the slow movement borrows from Jerome Kern, and the melodic material eventually turns into the opening of *Think only this*. The harmonies in the song are very simple, but in the concerto I wander (unnoticeably purposeful wandering, I hope) into Kern's world in an extended piano solo passage. The relationship between the soloist and the audience changes completely – a concerto soloist no longer, much more of a spontaneous entertainer; and when the orchestra comes in with a very sober, rather mediaeval, treatment of the first subject, my intention is that there's a feeling of loss, harmonically brought about.

There isn't a text, of course, but there's a principle. The word 'Concerto' implies a discussion, even an argument, between soloist and orchestra. So here, the piano tries to persuade the orchestra to share its material, and vice versa. The piano often pulls rank to interrupt the orchestra's bourgeois aspiration to symmetry. The other basic aspect of a concerto is that it displays virtuosity, and so I included a number of difficult technical devices that I happen to enjoy.

BN: It's interesting to learn that an improvisation around *Sea Pictures* kickstarted things. So perhaps that's where my ability to understand its musical language comes from – its relationship with Elgar. Are you in conversation with him a little here as well? I don't know where you've come closer to speaking with that particular musical hinterland.

DON: I don't think anyone would hear the opening as coming from *Sabbath Morning at Sea*, unless they knew its origin. The material is completely transformed, rather as Elgar transformed Rossini in his first recorded improvisation.

BN: What is it about *Sea Pictures* that made it a fit starting point for such a large undertaking as this? Why is that piece of importance? The love that ends, the love that goes away, the dream across the sea... all this is very rich, resonant material

Elgar's working with, and he handles it so soulfully. I think 'Where Corals Lie' in particular stays with me as so full of feeling. Were you hoping to access some of that?

DON: That song is certainly the hit of the cycle, but it wasn't in my mind. When I improvised my opening, I was simply musing on the further possibilities of an idea that Elgar had mused upon for twenty years. In his original polka it's a throwaway Coda. In his song, it's changed into a stately steamship. In my concerto, where the notes are different again, it's an urgent introduction that sets out the tonal argument, and usefully sets the tempo.

BN: You've worked on the piece on and off for the best part of your adult life. Is it the work you feel closest to? Perhaps it can't be the work you feel proudest of, having spent so much time with it, and taken it apart and put it back together again. It can't retain as much of its mystique.

DON: I'm proud of how it works, especially after my revisions to the slow movement. But I think you're right, I'm too familiar with it for it to surprise me. But I can still enjoy it, and it can surprise everyone else.

BN: Have you always been the soloist when this is performed?

DON: Always. I don't know how I'd feel about someone else playing it.

BN: Would it be your preference, ideally, to perform your own work, when premiered at least, or to conduct, or simply to listen?

DON: I enjoy performing my own work, but it's not always

possible. My last few premieres have not involved me on stage at all, and that's probably healthy.

*

Symphony was first performed on 24th May 2013 in Dorchester Abbey by the Orchestra of St. Paul's conducted by Ben Palmer, as part of the English Music Festival.

The revised version was first performed by the same artists in St. Paul's Church, Covent Garden on 1st October 2015.

I.   Air & Allegro

II.   March

III.   Adagio

IV.   Ground

*

BN: I have it in my mind that this is the work of which you're proudest.

DON: Yes. It answers a recurring question – what is a symphony? – to my own satisfaction.

BN: What can you tell us about the Symphony?

DON: It's about forty minutes long, and it's composed for a large orchestra stretching from piccolo to double-bassoon, with everything in between, including an Anvil, a Rain-Stick, and the rarely-heard Lion's Roar. It weaves together a host of musical references, from Joni Mitchell & the Beach Boys to Elizabethan lute-songs & the Art of Fugue. That musical mixture is refracted through prisms of cultural & scientific parallels: the mediaeval Elements of Fire, Air, Earth & Water, theories of Life, ideas of Birth & Bereavement, Hieronymus Bosch & Thomas Hardy, and the strange charm of Prime Numbers and of things that happen once – and never again.

BN: So how do these elements speak to each other? What was the thinking behind the juxtapositions you sought to make here? Or were they more or less spontaneous?

DON: They all relate to the theme of creation, of making things, literally what they're 'composed' of. The interesting task was to find out how these particular musical manifestations of that idea would react with each other when they were fitted together.

BN: Technically, the piece is quite an extensive extrapolation on quite a concentrated musical gesture.

DON: The piccolo's first six notes – which were another improvisation at first, with their accompanying chords – provide most of the musical material, and then there's an expanding wedge-shaped motive (which I think of as a representation of a double helix) and the folksong *Watkin's Ale*. Starting from the primeval simplicities of the Garden of Eden, the first two movements partly parallel the emotional path of Hardy's poem *A time there was*. The Adagio muses on the nature of creativity, ironically introducing that orchestral transcription of the sound of a photocopier. The finale finds salvation in the triumph of the human will. By a strange chance, the very day after I completed the Symphony, I came across James Lyon's powerful idea of Tune as Sonic Myth – the perfect verbal expression of some of my procedures.

BN: Could you outline that idea a little further?

DON: A myth/tune is beautiful and interesting in itself, but it contains multitudes of meanings. The meanings may be dry, expressed on their own, but clothed with the glamour of myth/tune, they are presented subtly, and each reader/listener can take their own shade of meaning.

BN: Was it always an ambition to write a Symphony? When does that interest date back to?

DON: I felt I was working up to it.

BN: Had you ever tried before?

DON: I'd tried to write a piano sonata in Paris – still haven't done that – but never a symphony, until the English Music Festival offered an orchestra.

BN: What can you tell us about the process of writing this piece?

DON: The movements are more closely related than in the Concerto. There, themes recur, and they all come together at the end, but in the Symphony the relationships are much more pervasive. I needed to keep the whole forty-minute shape in my mind at once, all the time, which was a wonderful feeling of total immersion. I felt the same thing later on, writing *HengeMusic*.

BN: Here, you're drawing very specifically on a folk song, *Watkin's Ale*, and more allusively on Hardy. So it feels like a moment to recapitulate some of the early themes of this book, and talk about Vaughan Williams and folk song collecting. Here, in this most confident of your pieces, you feel absolutely at ease with synthesising very different influences into a single music, and a great deal of what you draw together comes from the cultural hinterland we sought to establish for your thinking at the outset. Was this, in some part, a recapitulation of some of the places you felt you'd come from? And what was your interest in working with folk song here? It's obviously pleasing to juxtapose pub songs with this most exalted of musical forms – is that process of juxtaposition, which you've already mentioned, the key to the piece then?

DON: I came across *Watkin's Ale* quite recently, making a radio programme about Shakespeare. I was amazed I didn't know it – it takes the usual folksong seduction story and twists it, so the cocky young man finds himself out-lusted by his simple maiden. In the end, his will asserts itself, in a suitably Shakespearean manner. What's really interesting is how the tune tells the story all on its own, without the words. It was the perfect way to end a symphony about the processes of creation and corruption – to affirm that the human will can rise above it all. Making that point with a folk tune rooted everything in history.

Besides Hardy's poetry, I had those Blake engravings in mind – his particular visions of Behemoth, and the Sons of God dancing. All this is very exclusively English, of course, but it seemed the proper counterpart of the music I was writing. When I was an undergraduate, I was addicted to the engravings of

Doré and the visions of Bosch, but it's Blake that has stayed with me. I made settings of Wallace Stevens and Walt Whitman long ago, but it's Donne that remains. I've become more English as I go on, I suppose.

BN: What were the revisions you subsequently made, where did they come from?

DON: I mentioned the charm of things that happen once, and never again. The second subject of the first movement was one of those, but it was really too important for that. And the very end of the symphony seemed to me a bit too abrupt. Bringing back the second subject just before the coda solved both problems. It works in particular because I'm already revisiting first movement material at this point in the piece.

BN: As well as being a piece you were happy with yourself, I also remember you being very happy with the responses. This is one of the great pleasures of making things, I think – the conversations you create, and are then able to take forwards, out of the idea that you had. Were there conversations that opened up new ground off the back of this work? I'm imagining that people's responses must be particularly rich and varied where a piece doesn't have a text to channel all reactions?

DON: People responded to the piece in a new way. They were all convinced that it carried ideas, even a philosophy. That's what I think a symphony should do, so the responses pleased me. In my work, people are normally responding to words in the first instance, so the ideas in the music can be neglected. In my other instrumental piece, the Concerto, listeners find pleasure and beauty in all sorts of things, but few penetrate – or feel the need to penetrate – to its philosophy. With the symphony I managed to cross that barrier, and that was something I bore in mind when I came to write *HengeMusic*.

*

STERNE, was THE MAN was first performed on 14th October 2013 in York Minster by children from local schools, the York String Quartet, David Bradley (actor), Mark Wilde (tenor), Susanna Pell (viola da gamba) and the composer (square piano) conducted by Jon Brigg.

*

BN: This piece has a lovely story behind it, the route to com-missioning is quite different to what we've examined so far. To date, we've discussed self-generated pieces, and collaborations with the English Music Festival, but this was the product of a different friendship, at a different end of the country, and also an approach from a different artistic medium that acted as a bridge between written and musical cultures, where your piece sits.

DON: It was another phone call out of the blue. Patrick Wildgust rang and introduced himself as the curator of Shandy Hall, Laurence Sterne's former vicarage in Coxwold, about twenty miles north of York. Our first collaborations were concerts of music relating to Sterne, on square piano. Next, we drove round Yorkshire rescuing and redistributing square pianos.

Then Patrick had the idea of a musical setting of a sermon.

BN: It's good to hear how sometimes things arise from friend-ships and synchronicities and unexpected approaches in this way. What was the outline of Patrick's commission?

DON: It was to be Sterne's last sermon, The Case of Hezekiah & the Messengers, which grapples with the moral problem of doing the right thing for the wrong reason, set for children's choirs (which Patrick specially formed for the occasion from the villages round Coxwold), viola da gamba (because the great gambist C.F. Abel used to improvise during readings of Sterne), plus an actor and a tenor. And square piano, of course. We added in a string quartet and a natural trumpet – all instruments that Sterne would have known.

During his lifetime, Sterne's sermons were as famous as his novels, and the Trust's commission was intended to draw attention to a neglected literary form. The piece ends with a setting of the epitaph on Sterne's gravestone, now in the porch of Coxwold church. My title is taken from the couplet:

> *STERNE, was THE MAN, who with gigantic stride*
> *Mowed down luxuriant follies, far and wide*

BN: And what can you say about the work produced?

DON: The music was composed in the conviction that inexpe-rienced children are perfectly capable of singing complicated rhythms in a high tessitura – which proved to be the case. I found some details of the harmonic language for the two recitatives for tenor and viola da gamba by applying contemporary cello techniques to the distinctive tuning of the gamba's six strings. I used rounds and ostinatos to aid the children's memory. The *Virtues & Vices* movement combines ostinato and refrain, a technique I developed much further in *HengeMusic*. Here, the mirror pitches of the ostinato represent humanity's vacillation between good and evil, continually rising above middle C and falling below it – CDCDCBABAB. That's where the phrase 'we want not to *be*, but to *seem*' comes in.

BN: 'Drawing attention to a neglected literary form' is a cause close to my heart, I must say. And it's not unlike what I think you try to do when you write for the organ, or play the organ, which I think probably has to qualify as a neglected instrument these days.

It's interesting to think about what one chooses to write about, advocate, draw attention to. I think it's Addison who argues a critic should draw attention to the excellences in an artist; a radical view when you think how many journalists commit their lives to chronicling the iniquities of the world. I think we both share an interest in trying to give oxygen to the under-appreciated. I'm thinking of the fact that no-one had set the Prayer Book before – doing so is a way of asking people to actually look at the words in it, not simply to read them out.

I've thought long and hard since I started to write non-fiction like this as to what I'm trying to draw attention to. The short pieces I write for newspapers and magazines are mainly sketches really, just ways of drafting thoughts – some of them quite useful, perhaps even interesting, to me at least, but all just sketches. Writing this book and the book I wrote about Peter Gill are very different undertakings though. My process in both cases has been to take the life and work of someone who I know well, and whose work I know very well, and to write the first book that's ever been written about them. And it has occurred to me that if I kept going long enough, perhaps one day I'd be able to get a uniform edition published called 'In Defence Of Lost Causes'!

Sorry, rude, I know. But for all that that's a glib line, it's also the reason I think I'm interested in certain people more than others – some people's work does get lost, despite being just as valid or interesting or valuable as the work of other people who are widely studied. Sometimes people's work gets lost precisely because it's more interesting, in fact. So it's interesting to try and draw attention to artists whose work, to my mind, demands more attention.

DON: Peter Gill and I are fortunate to have your attention. These days, with electronic media so capacious, I don't think much will be lost for ever, provided it's sincere work. Over the years, I've broadcast or recorded lost pieces by dozens of composers. Most of them are still very much niche interests, but there's always a cadre of enthusiasts. And sometimes it goes beyond that. My friend Lewis Foreman has spent his life reviving lost composers – perhaps his biggest success is Arnold Bax, whose music is now mostly recorded. He's not really famous, of course. Even Parry is known for only one piece. But I don't think either of them was composing for fame; and at least nowadays, people who want to engage with Bax's mind or Parry's mind can do so. It's taken about a hundred years of cumulative effort.

BN: It occurs to me that these odd and brilliant men of letters who have appeared from time to time in the history of letters rather suit your tastes – Dr Johnson is an interest of yours, and Donne, and also Sterne. All polyglot, magpie brains, working across many forms, all torn in the way Matthew Arnold was between having fun and doing good, perhaps.

Your commitment to work with young people has lasted throughout your working life. Beginning with teaching work at the junior Academy, it's now developed into university teaching and professorial appointments and associate positions at half the conservatoires in the country. But I've noticed that it's also always manifested itself as a sense of responsibility around working with school age children – leading workshops, writing pieces, making yourself available to people at the very beginning of thinking about music. Is that civic responsibility? Or is it a way of being in touch with that aspect of yourself, or funding, or what?

DON: It's paying back what people did for me so generously when I was a child – all those piano teachers and school-mistresses and vicars and choirmasters. They shared their interests with me, and I share my interests with young people so that certain ways of listening to the world can carry on. Subtly adapted to their times, of course! Chances to work with schoolchildren are much rarer than they were – so many forms to fill in, so many other demands on the teachers' time – so the Sterne Trust commission was very welcome. Some people thought it would be too hard for the children to sing, but it turned out that if you don't make a great fuss about how difficult something is, children are fine.

BN: This, I think, was the first time your soloist was a non-musician. What was the thinking behind working with the great David Bradley?

DON: Patrick wanted a Yorkshire voice of Sternean authority, and David certainly has that. And he entered into the part – there's a sort of recklessness about his personality that Sterne must have had too, so it was very convincing when David was bellowing out his gnomic anathemas in the Quire of York Minster, where Sterne himself would have sat so often.

BN: It's worth saying, though, that working with actors in concerts has been something you've done quite a bit of, outside your own work.

DON: Audiences love programmes of poems and songs. When I worked at the RSC, David Wilson-Johnson and I used to do Hardy and Housman with Peter Clough, who was Silvius in the RSC *As You Like It* I played in so often. It was about that time that I first worked with Gabriel Woolf, performing what are technically called melodramas, for speaker and piano, like Poulenc's *Babar the Elephant* or Richard Strauss's *Enoch Arden*. Timothy West and I did a Sitwell programme or two, where we fitted Sacheverell's words to Debussy as background music. We did Walton's *Façade*, with Prunella Scales as well, of course – great party piece of theirs. Christopher Benjamin has performed my Sterne piece a couple of times. And I was the music quizmaster for a BBC2 series pitting Simon Callow against John Sessions, which opened the door for me to ask them to join in with other things – Dickens things with Simon, melodrama with John. I've learned a lot from actors.

BN: What did you take from this time spent with Sterne's sermons? Is the rest of Sterne of interest to you?

DON: I've caught up with a lot of Sterne now, and it's actually the sermons that I find most interesting. The eighteenth-century church is sneered at a good deal, but Sterne preached that last sermon of his to a congregation that included David Hume, and he rose to the challenge. Fascinating to try to work out how his mind was working – a bit like Donne.

BN: One thing that stays with you from hearing the piece is your experimenting with rhythm again, your interest in syncopation and the dance of rhythm. I think this may be quite a jazz-influenced piece, a certain type of jazz that Lambert might have been taking in as well. The Mayerl end of the spectrum.

DON: Billy Mayerl did himself no favours when he wrote, in his piano tutor, about 'Jazz … a word which we hate, by the way.' But his acknowledgment that he was no jazzer reminds us of what he was – the subtle stylist of the syncopated novelty. Not so very different from George Gershwin, except in the matter of ambition and scale. Gershwin dealt in operas and concertos and musicals. Mayerl abandoned the three-minute piano piece only for an unsuccessful symphonic poem. Yet his piano pieces and song transcriptions, and their brilliant technical tricks and devices, are streets ahead of Gershwin's. And his tunes aren't far behind, both songs and piano pieces, though his collaboration with Enid Blyton shows Ira Gershwin in an extremely flattering light. Purely technically, there's quite a lot of Mayerl in my Piano Concerto.

STERNE, was THE MAN owes more to Lambert, as you

suggest. Lambert immediately grasped the rhythmic possibilities that could be developed from certain aspects of jazz. He saw how the syncopations of secondary rag, and the way that early jazz composers like Arndt or Confrey used to run a four-note rhythm round their five fingers till it all matched up again, could result in irregular time signatures and irrational ostinatos – you hear that straight away at the beginning of *Rio Grande*. I work with those ideas all through my Symphony, and in quite a lot of *STERNE*, which was written more or less at the same time.

BN: That rhythmic focus in your work may also have its roots, it occurs to me, in the way you write. In my experience, you have two main methods of writing music – whistling, and humming. And the humming is much more about shape and less melodic, while the whistling is much more melodic and looser in shape. I've recently been given quite a serious talking to by my wife, because while finishing this book and thinking about your work a lot, I've started imitating your method of composing-by-humming round the flat – which is basically to wander round doing housework whilst saying 'rig-a-dig-ba-da-bam' in a Schoenbergian drone. I imagine you probably do some more technical stuff as well! This piece, I suspect, was mostly written by humming?

DON: I had no idea I did that! In my defence, I can claim that the noises are merely the extraneous symptoms of internal thought. But I think you're right, there are two aspects to the thinking, and *STERNE* is mostly humming.

*

Turning Points was first performed on 19th September 2015 in St. Mary's Church Southampton by Southampton University Symphony Orchestra (SUSO), Southampton University Brass Band (SUBB), the New London Chamber Choir, Highcliffe Junior Choir, Amanda Pitt (soprano), Mark Wilde (tenor) & Peter Savidge (baritone), conducted by Joe Beckhelling. The piece was commissioned by Agincourt 600.

Turning Points: Fantasia upon a suffragist song by Sir Hubert Parry

I.   Battles & Manifestos

II.   Lament

III.   Boney

IV.   Malala

V.   Gettysburg

VI.   Finale

*

BN: Here's a project that takes all the more creative and eclectic and playful elements of *Prayerbook* and *STERNE, was THE MAN* and develops them significantly. Give us an outline of *Turning Points*.

DON: *Turning Points* is a Celebration of Democracy, with especial reference to the events of 1215 (Magna Carta), 1415 (Agincourt) & 1815 (Waterloo). The libretto draws upon Magna Carta itself, contemporary accounts of Agincourt, the American

Declaration of Independence, Robert Burns's *A man's a man for a' that*, the despatches of the Duke of Wellington (the first time the Duke's words have been set to music), & the Gettysburg Address. It includes the words of Sir Winston Churchill, Martin Luther King & Malala Yousafzai, and it features the rhythmic chant of an angry crowd in Ferguson, Missouri, which I jotted down from a radio news bulletin in November 2014. The key sentences in the libretto are 'The annals of earlier reigns should have served as lesson for the lords of France' and 'The price of liberty is eternal vigilance'.

Musically, the whole piece is a Fantasia on Sir Hubert Parry's 1912 unison song *You'll get there*. The prominent suffragist Millicent Garrett Fawcett, a close family friend of Parry's, quotes its second verse as the epigraph to the 1912 chapter of her book *The Women's Victory*. The poem, written by 'The Trent Otter' (J.W. Martin), and published in *The Fishing Gazette*, was perhaps brought to Parry's attention by his son-in-law, the celebrated baritone and even more famous fisherman, Harry Plunkett Greene. This is the first of a series of unison songs in a popular style that Parry produced towards the end of his life: a stylistic development that may have led to more *Jerusalem*s were it not for the influenza epidemic of 1918. For this reason, as well as its political context, *You'll get there* is well worth developing through a long piece.

BN: So here we see the product of your developing interests – having spent a lot of time with Elgar, you moved on to Parry, and started trying to engage with his work in your own.

DON: I've studied a lot of Parry very deeply in the last few years, and I've begun to work out what makes his music tick. There are possibilities within it which he had no time to develop – rather like Lambert.

BN: The other composer who looms over this enterprise is William Walton.

DON: Although the piece uses all three '15 anniversaries to focus its political message, it was commissioned by Agincourt 600, so its first performance was at a concert that included Walter Leigh's *Agincourt* Overture and Walton's *Henry V* music, with Hasan Dixon – another fine actor. As a result, one factor in my mind was that I needed to sound rather different from Walton, though his celebratory style is very infectious.

BN: Yes, the idea of the piece as being in conversation with Walton, rather than being in his music's debt, seems right to me. This, it's worth noting, is a piece that also came from a new commissioning relationship. Despite this, it feels more like a cohering of themes and preoccupations in your work into a new clarity of focus. It develops certain key preoccupations in your work – choral singing, the setting of unexpected texts, the juxtaposition of cultures, ideas and arguments, the role of history as a part of our now. From what you say, I wonder whether it was also the same kind of allusive response to present events that you've revealed *Think only this* to be – did the situation in Ferguson initiate aspects of this work, and send you back to suffragism and these other turning points?

DON: The idea of finding a political thread that links Magna Carta, Agincourt and Waterloo came up in conversation with

Mark Wilde, who was involved with Lincoln Cathedral's Magna Carta celebrations. My friend Anne Curry, the great expert on Agincourt, had been wondering about the possibility of a musical celebration too; and then there were conversations with another friend, Josephine Oxley, who is the curator of Apsley House, the Duke of Wellington's house – Number One, London. Once Anne had shown me the speech that the Lord Chancellor – who was Henry's uncle and Bishop of Winchester as well – made to Parliament in autumn 1414, I realized the sort of texts I needed. He was asking for money, and without it, Henry could never have gone to war. The idea of parliamentary approval of war has become acute for us in the present century. I searched for words that similarly leapt out of their own time, and became real for us now. I didn't want to write a piece that would only work in 2015 – I needed to universalise the story. The Burns was an obvious place to start, and the suffragettes brought Malala Yousafzai very much to mind. Contemporary descriptions of the carnage at Agincourt cast a light on the Duke's despatch concerning the bloodiest battle ever fought, up to that time, and the geography of Waterloo hinted at still bloodier battles a century later. From the time I started compiling my libretto I was even more aware of politics than usual. I read the Declaration of Independence on a sign on Boston Common during a trip to America, and I followed the story of Ferguson very closely – though I'd already conceived the piece by then.

BN: It's also a recapitulation of your interest in writing about war, as *Think only this* had already seen you do.

DON: War is so terrible that it cannot be ignored. And it

produces interesting words – not just the words of great orators like Lincoln or Churchill, but the complicated responses of French poets or English generals. Setting Wellington's despatches to music was a fascinating study – I had to find the rhythms of his mind.

While I was writing the piece, I found myself playing the piano that Blüthners sent to Neville Chamberlain in 1938 in gratitude for averting war. That was one reason I wrote a prominent piano duet part – my initial hope was to have it played by political pianists like William Hague, Alan Rusbridger or James Naughtie, but Lord Hague's courteous but very well-reasoned refusal got rid of that idea!

BN: I suppose the interesting thing in a juxtaposition of *Think only this* and *Turning Points* is the vast difference in formal invention and creative freedom that exists between the two pieces. Which I don't intend as a qualitative judgement at all, but I hope you'll go with me – *Turning Points*, while it actually has a very supple, gently modulated musical identity, a coherence that stems from its always interrogating Parry, is also in some ways like a Matisse cut-out. The effect might be simple and clean but the process of making is really very eclectic. Picasso and Braque and Matisse were not references springing to mind when I was thinking about the song cycles, but they very much are here.

DON: That's good that the piece has its own identity. The kaleidoscopic nature of the music matches the patchwork of the libretto. The first movement gradually sets out the whole of Parry's tune, heavily disguised, and also the premises of the piece, which are then commented upon in shorter movements which give the opportunity for various meditations on the tune. The technical challenge was making the music flow through the libretto, as it were. The quotations are arranged as a stream of consciousness, and the music needs to suit each 'voice', but also to have its own coherence.

BN: How did you go about the process of selecting material for this piece? And how did you bring it all together in the writing?

DON: I chose key texts from the three anniversaries, and used them to set out the basic premises of the long first movement, shining lights on them with interleaved texts from other centuries, other countries. Then the meditations follow. *Lament* has the piano duet mesmerically repeating Parry's first six notes, representing the psychological 'fugue state' in which the Agincourt war-widow finds herself, while the flute and the soprano soloist play with the Agincourt Carol. *Boney* is three things – a scherzo, a folk-tune, and a history lesson – but it's bound into the piece as the splendidly strenuous tune is revealed as a counterpoint to the all-pervasive music I made for Drayton's 'Fair stood the wind for France' in the first movement. *Malala* uses words so emblematic that I only needed seven of them: 'I am Malala' and 'I have a dream'. There's a marvellous onomatopoeic Ghandian passive resistance about these words, and the children's choir sings them to a gently stubborn ostinato on Parry's first four notes. The final sections of the piece are recapitulations that reveal Wellington and Lincoln as blood-brothers in more ways than just sharing a soloist. At last we hear the Parry tune clearly for the first time – the fantasy has attained the reality. Its choral presentation is first achieved by democratic, wordless whistling rather than by singing words in any particular language. And finally, three melodies are combined: the Burns folk-tune, 'Fair stood the wind', and Parry. A simple political point about combination.

BN: The very exciting outcome from the first performance of this piece was a genuine popular response from its audience. This interests me as a potential breakthrough. You've told that excellent story about the middle-aged white man from the south east asking whether the plan was to shoot everyone like him, but it's important to say that that doesn't quite wash, in the end – music, as you have ceaselessly worked to achieve, ought to be for everyone. I know you know that. But this piece I think seemed to engage a wider demographic of listener than some of the work you've made that takes more traditional musical shapes.

DON: I wrote a piece in the *Guardian* about Political Rhythms, and Neville Chamberlain's grand-daughter very kindly let me tell the story of the Blüthner on the *Today* programme. The predominantly youthful performers brought their own support organisations, and it was an official Agincourt event. So lots of people came who don't go to many choral concerts, and they all absolutely got it. The audience at the premiere was quite anarchic – people pinched the reserved VIP seats, so the entry of Lords Mayor, Spiritual and Temporal was attended by a great scraping together of extra chairs from the church hall. I found myself sitting next to members of the Occupy movement – we had Giles Fraser as a mutual friend – and they really enjoyed it.

BN: This was a piece, I think, that took an enormous amount of organising to bring these many different elements together. Do you like playing that Binkie Beaumont impresario role, and being the one who has to tear the tickets? Does that form part of the pleasure of it all for you?

DON: My budgets often mean that I'm not putting on concerts in fully equipped and staffed concert halls. No-one else was going to move the pews around for *Turning Points*. I'm trying to jettison some of this work. But as for ticket-tearing, I like to meet my audiences, and that won't change.

*

HengeMusic for saxophone quartet and organ, with films by Rob Lambert and poems by Barney Norris, was first performed on 29th October 2015 in the Chapel of Keble College, Oxford, by Sarah Baldock (organ), John Harle, Rob Buckland, Paul Stevens & Andy Findon (saxophones) and Barney Norris (speaker).

I: **Winter**

Entrance, Pavane & Galliard, Rounds, and Chorale Prelude

II: **Spring**

Fugue

III: **Summer**

Birdsong, Toccata, Midsummer Chorale, and Lullaby

IV: **Tango**

upon the folksong 'Once I had a sprig of thyme'

V: **Autumn**

Ostinato

VI: **The Thirteenth Moon**

Distance

*

BN: Then we come to *HengeMusic*, the piece to which I contributed poems, that we toured together with an organist and a saxophone quartet in 2015. Another piece for organ, interestingly. Saxophone quartet, though, is a very unexpected juxtaposition. How did that come about?

DON: Two reasons: in the right hands, the saxophone can attain a primeval quality that makes it the perfect instrument for prehistory; and secondly, as soon as I imagined it, I just knew a sax quartet would sound fantastic with organ.

BN: *HengeMusic* is a piece that was years in growing, as you visited the site you were writing about a great many times over many years, also because of an organ.

DON: I was organist at Poole Parish Church for some years, so every Sunday I drove past the amazing place that gave me the idea.

BN: Could you outline the piece for us?

DON: It's an hour-long multi-media experience rooted in English landscape. It shows the passage of the seasons at Knowlton Rings in Dorset, a neolithic henge with a ruined Norman church at its centre. At the ceremonial entrance to the henge stands a yew grove, still a place of prayer, as the ribbons, favours and photographs hanging from the branches firmly attest. The piece explores the abiding importance of the human quest for spiritual meaning.

The turning seasons are reflected in the cyclic musical procedures of the piece – variation, rondo, fugue, and, in *Autumn*, a development of the ostinato/refrain form used in the *Virtues & Vices* movement of *STERNE, was THE MAN*. The organ represents the landscape and the forces of nature, while the saxophones represent human agency and intelligence, sometimes expressed by their use of twelve-note techniques against the organ's often modal backdrop. This opposition is also expressed through bitonality – two keys at once – usually between saxes and organ, but occasionally within the sax group itself, most noticeably at the beginning of the *Tango*, where the soprano sax enters a fifth too high. The folksong remembered in the *Tango*, *A sprig of thyme*, is slightly altered to bring it closer to the ostinato figure used in the succeeding movement.

BN: This piece intensifies a sense that over the last few years you've been moving away from traditional musical structures – the song cycles and the concerto or symphony form – towards freer ideas about form that allow you to do whatever you feel you need for the piece.

DON: The conventional forms of classical music usually reach a conclusion. Audiences usually want a conclusion, of course, so I provide one even for oddly shaped pieces like *STERNE* or *Turning Points*, neither of which really concludes – Sterne does not present what David Jenkins would call 'a knock-down miracle'; the march to democracy continues. But in *HengeMusic* I needed to make an ouroboros, the snake that eats its own tail as a symbol of infinity. Schumann did that in his song cycle *Dichterliebe*, but it's pretty rare. I have a hope that one day I can bring the ouroboros aspect – the seasonal aspect – to the fore, by having the piece played six times in succession by three different organists and two different saxophone quartets, in all the possible combinations. Each performance would be different, just as six successive autumns are different, but it would all be the same piece, just as the six autumns would all be autumn.

BN: And yet you're still playing with traditional elements – with folk songs extrapolated, for example. This is 'tradition and change' playing out the tension between each other again.

DON: A distorted memory of an Elizabethan Pavan and Galliard, each a variation on a variation, a series of receding mirrors, near the beginning. A distorted memory of a folk-song, near the end.

BN: Something that strikes me as quite courageous, in this piece, is the absolutely tie-died nature of the material. It doesn't particularly sound like hippy art, but comes across it when reasoned through ever so slightly as something Fairport Convention or 60s Joni Mitchell wouldn't have done because it was too far-out. Do you think that says something about contemporary spirituality? It might be possible to engage with it in a specifically Christian context, but it seems to want to exist in a broader frame of references.

DON: It's not a specifically Christian piece. We don't know many of the details of the religion of the people who dug the henge, but we're sure they had religion. We may not be very close to the Normans who forcibly pacified the spirits of the henge by building a church in it, perhaps with its own dolmens, just as they pacified the Saxons by building castles. I'm probably not very close to the people who hang ribbons and poems from the yew branches. But we've all shared a spiritual attraction to this particular spot. I don't know whether the yews were hung with mementos in years gone by, but seventy-five years ago American servicemen were carving their names on the ruins, so perhaps spirituality nowadays is more inclusive than it was then, at least.

BN: The piece came with quite a few bells and whistles – another non-actor soloist who read material; and for the first time, video projection. Just as eclectic an approach to making work as *Turning Points*. It's here that I really started noticing that you came from the same generation as McBurney. The piece, like *Turning Points*, has an interest in playing with things that create cool effects that can be useful to the project that is very like Complicite's work.

DON: You reading your poems was a wonderful way of re-gearing the listeners' minds around each of the four sections. The films came about through a chance meeting at the henge with someone else who loves the place, Rob Lambert. We got chatting, and it turned out he's a professional photographer with the inestimable advantage of living just down the road. So he started to film the henge in all weathers and all seasons: the one day in years that there was snow, he was there just after dawn. A lucky meeting indeed. It was interesting to work out ways in which the films (of invariable length) could fit with the live music, which varied in length according to how the acoustic favoured the sax quartet and the organ – not to mention your readings. Luckily, organists are used to tailoring their music to fit a given bit of speech.

BN: Cyclical time and the return of the seasons brings us back, perhaps, to the metaphysical preoccupations discernible in your work on Donne. What were you interested in exploring here?

DON: After spirituality, landscape – but a musician always works in the medium of time, so I found a way of seeing landscape through time; seasons, and prehistoric process. There's an idea that Englishness in music is all about landscape. I don't particularly share that idea – Smetana's Czech landscape pieces don't sound very English to me, and neither my symphony nor my concerto have anything to do with landscape, yet people think they sound English. But the idea is persistent enough for me to want to see what would happen to my music if I tried to make it about landscape. Then I was interested in the contrast between the inevitable processes of nature and the urgent self-interest of mankind – hence religion, I suppose – and hence the saxophones.

BN: And can I ask, bearing in mind the epigraph of the piece, how it was changed and shaped by the death of your father, which was happening while you were finishing the music, and had just happened when we were playing it? That must have impacted on what you were doing.

DON: The dedication is 'For my mother and father ... and theirs ... and theirs ...', which sums up the cyclical nature of human existence. My father was admitted to hospital with a broken hip just as the piece was hurtling towards its completion. The day he died, I went home and wrote the chorale prelude which turns into the climax of the piece, the Midsummer Chorale, where the midday sun shrieks through the window of the roofless tower like a searchlight, haloed against the summer sky, as the saxophones and the organ vie with each other to see who can make the loudest acclamation. I associate this section with the Raising of Lazarus – one inspiration for it was the eleventh-century alabaster bas-relief in Chichester Cathedral. The Toccata was conceived as the reverse of a dance of death, with the Biblical valley of bones in mind – *Dem bones, dem bones, dem – dry bones*, as the spiritual puts it. And during it, you'll recall, Rob Lambert's film of the ruin undergoes a great transformation, as it morphs into a precisely similar church nearby, that is *not* in ruins. Then, during the Lullaby, everything decays again, and we're at the nub of the piece. The organ falls silent, and the saxophones – mankind – are left alone to make what sense they can of Time. Typically of mankind, the folksong proposes a playful intellectualisation of the problem – a pun, no less.

Once I had a sprig of thyme...

Thyme it is a precious thing

And thyme it will grow on

> And thyme it'll bring all things to an end
>
> And so does my thyme grow on.

At which point the organ returns, the Tango gives way to less rational rhythms, and finally the full moon rises to a valedictory recomposition of the opening music.

BN: On the day when we played the piece closest to Knowlton, we all went out to look at the stone circle and the ruined church and the place we were making all the fuss about, and we hadn't quite clocked that it was the autumnal equinox. It was one of the more extraordinary events of my life.

DON: It was Halloween too. The Dorset Grove of Druids was there in force. There seemed to be a sacrificial couple clad in white, and a shaman in a crow's-feather cloak. Most of us hung well back, wondering what on earth we were about to witness – watched too many Midsomer Murders, I dare say – but you went and investigated! Nice chaps?

BN: I had a nice chat with an initially wary gent named Dave, who warmed to me once I didn't laugh at him or try and nick his drum. I think he'd been posted as a lookout at the edge of the ceremony to ward off feral youth. He took the time to explain the occasion to me, and let me know how much longer it would last. What was interesting was observing that it was neither more nor less serious and po-faced than the Christian services I've experienced. It looked very outlandish and one's first thoughts do tend in the direction of *The Wicker Man* upon encountering someone dressed in crow feathers singing what sounds like Gaelic, but really, Dave was singing along with the songs and following the routine, but still happy to break off and speak to me in the way that someone in a church pew will break off to say something to their partner, or check their children are all right. There's a tendency to assume that more niche pursuits or, in this case, faiths might attract more fervent individuals, aware that they're making an unusual choice in their cultural context and having to commit twice as passionately as a result, but this was just ritual, like many other rituals. Neither more or less mumbo-jumbo attached to it than a Sunday morning in a cathedral, a Saturday night in a theatre, an evening in a concert hall, etc. In fact, there was even one bloke who kept popping behind the church to vape throughout the ceremony we observed! Which reminded me of every lay clerk I've met.

*

BN: That takes us up to the present moment, of course, the sum of the work we've been talking about throughout this book. So, let me ask you – what are you working on next? Listening to your work in order to be able to ask you these questions, I've been struck that what's happening is a steady unmooring from the formal structures so much of your repertoire as a performer sticks to, and a progressively more ambitious approach to orchestration and subject matter. That is offset by certain abiding interests – the folk culture spun into art, the interplay between tradition and change, permanence and change, that makes all the work very spiritual whether it's formally religious or not. And formal playfulness and wit, I think, are contexts. So what do we have to look forward to?

DON: Your summation of my preoccupations is bang on. What next? I have quantities of sketches – including most of a versified libretto – that will become *The Body in the Ballroom*. A game of Cluedo for four characters, one deceased. More playful than spiritual, perhaps, but opera gives scope for psychological depth, even an opera for three voices and piano.

BN: *The Body In The Ballroom* is a long-cherished project, while the other piece you're planning, *Clare's Fiddle*, is something you've only started thinking about more recently, I think?

DON: I made a radio programme at John Clare's cottage in Helpston a few years ago, for which I read through his manuscript folk-fiddle collection and his transcriptions of the folksongs sung to him by his mother and father. It's led to a re-reading of his poetry. More recently, experiences like broadcasting *The Lark Ascending* on Vaughan Williams's own piano, and a television thing on Holst and folk-music, have started to whirl about with my Clare ideas, waiting for me to synthesize them into something that will crystallize my mind. Folksong and landscape again, at first blush, but it'll be very different from *HengeMusic*. I've been developing technical processes based on John Barrell's analysis of temporal conjunctions in Clare's poetry.

BN: Both pieces are returns to places from your past – Sussex, and Northampton. Is that something you're conscious of?

DON: My interest in Clare started because we share a county, but it's moved on from that. *The Body in the Ballroom* is not really a Sussex piece, except that I wrote the song I'll use to symbolise the ballroom while I was living at Petworth – it's a setting of an amusing unpublished poem Roger McGough gave me, *The Marquis de Sade Waltz*. It made a few concert appearances back in the 90s, and I think it went out on the radio, but the tune has possibilities that I didn't know how to explore back then.

BN: We've come to the end, and spent a great many pages trying to lay out some of the territory your work traverses, and I feel keenly the inadequacy of all attempts like this to put things into words, to do any more than scratch the surface. I suppose, as we finish this section, the last thing I'd do in trying to do justice to this book's initial goals would be to ask you how you'd want listeners to your work to approach these pieces, how you hope people will meet them?

DON: What I'd most like is for people to listen to the music more than once. And if something begins to mean something to them, I'd hope they might share it with their friends.

Epilogue

David Owen Norris's life is an unfinished gesture, so these movements we've constructed perhaps inevitably end up feeling unresolved when we come to the end of them. Like Alfred Hitchcock's *The Birds*, or Angela Carter's *The Magic Toyshop*, like Moses looking out over the promised land, we seem to have been brought all this way, only to have reached a point from which the story seems ready to really begin. There is something abrupt about concluding a survey of the work of someone who still has more work to make. It's thrilling, in one sense, to address ideas that are still in the process of developing, but it does mean a book such as this must of necessity have an open ending. It is throwing a conversation forwards, rather than wrapping it up. There will be more to say every time another new work emerges.

Perhaps one danger that always arises with books like this is that they feel like journeys away from a centre. They set out to explore certain preoccupations, but the tension between fidelity to a theme and fidelity to the course of the life in question means the ideas under the surface of the story flit in and out of focus, because that's what life is like. People don't confront the themes that define their lives head on. They live, and the meanings creep up on them. So I'm aware this book has been an exploration of the undergrowth of certain ideas, not a systematic survey of the ideas themselves, in accordance with that reality. We have ambled, and wandered, and wondered aloud.

But in the end, I think that's how a lot of books about art come out. Art doesn't look at its subjects head on either, not if it's any good. I've always considered it a decent rule of thumb

that if you can express the meaning of a play in a line of dialogue then the play isn't worth writing, because it's not a play at
all, it's a line. In that way, Dad's interest in Donne has always
resonated with me. His pleasure in the unstable relationship
between art and experience, the ambiguity of the poetry, is
exactly what I prize in my favourite artistic work. It's the same
thing I've always found interesting in Dad's Anglicanism, too –
a commitment to the merits of philosophical ambiguity, perhaps
even of ironic detachment. I can't persuade myself into a
religion, and never have been able to, but I admire that aspect
of the Anglican worldview. Which, I suppose, is what we've been
discussing all this time.

A work of art takes the form of a journey out. An exploration
away from some real or imagined centre. That's their job – to
drag us away from what we know, to keep us enquiring, and stop
us growing stagnant and too self-assured. That's why books like
this tend to follow a similar pattern. They're studying things that
have to be reaching into the unknown in order to have real
value. I don't know, really, whether they arrive anywhere, these
explorations, except that they go on their journey, and they
finish. That's why they're like life, of course – they go on their
journeys, and who can tell whether or not they get anywhere, or
whether it was all just the sound of time passing? Each of us has
to decide that for ourselves, when we've finished the story, when
we've listened to the music.

But perhaps that's what I think because I don't have a
religion.

I conclude this book with the obscure sense that there is more
to say, but I have to accept that I'm not the person who will say
it. The further statements will be made by the composer, in the

music he goes on to write, by readers and listeners who go on to experience this work, and by other critics, more able than I, who will perhaps find this volume useful as a starting point. I hope these conversations go some way towards offering a resonant context for listening to Dad's music. An appendix detailing the recordings available is included at the back of this book. They are the record of a mind following its own tracks, and that is rare, and it is fascinating. I hope I have shared some of my own delight at what they have to give.

The other thing I hope I've done over the course of this book, by asserting that this work exists, has merit, deserves attention, is to argue in my own allusive way for the inherent validity of any reasoned voice, any cultural perspective, no matter how it sits within the main stream of our cultural discourse. It's been Dad's fate to make much of his music away from the contemporary centres of our musical culture. In this country, that can too often be interpreted as an indicator of quality, and that needs to be challenged. It isn't true, and if it were allowed to be true, it would be boring and perhaps even dangerous. In the past, this has been an island where people strove to assert the equal dignity and value of every life, whether or not it was spent at the centre. It was D.H. Lawrence, after all, who wrote a scene in his first play *A Collier's Friday Night* where a young man tells a young woman who doesn't think she's good enough for him, and fears she bores him, 'as much happens for you as happens for other people'. England may be burdened by a history of cultural repression and homogenising unrivalled even by the Roman Empire, but it has been other things as well – it has been the wellspring of the labour movement, the well-spring of universal suffrage, the wellspring of that Lawrentian respect for every person. It is in those chapters of the country's history that I believe a tolerant and pluralistic future waits to be discovered.

But it's the job of all of us to draw attention to those qualities, however we can, and be always attentive to the way the past is used to shape the future. Because people need the artists who stick out at odd angles, and don't fit the mould, and don't want to ask the questions there are funding incentives in place to support – we need people who want to journey away from the centre, or we revert to the mean every time. When the National Theatre staged a mash-up of Lawrence's plays called *Husbands and Sons* in 2016, the line I've just quoted was cut. I thought it highly significant that it could be considered dispensable, a telling reflection of the culture we live in, where likes and shares and views do change a person's value, where search algorithms do narrow our frames of reference and funnel us all into the same preoccupations. There have been periods in the century since Lawrence wrote that line where it would have been considered indispensable – a distillation, in fact, of everything Lawrence stood for. (You could even argue that if he'd followed my rule of thumb, he shouldn't have written the play.) That's been a part of the story of England from time to time. In directing attention for a little while to this work, the music of David Owen Norris, which hasn't quite flowered unseen, as Grey would have it, but has nonetheless been heard echoing some way away from the centre we've built for ourselves, I hope I've been asserting the value of continuing to prize Lawrence's crucial sentiment, and making our journeys out, as we travel on into the future.

Appendix

Compositions by David Owen Norris

Think only this, song cycle, 2002
(available from EM Records, EMR CD015)

Tomorrow nor Yesterday, song cycle, 2006-13
(available from EM Records, EMR CD0015)

Prayerbook, an oratorio about tradition and change, 2006
(available from EM Records, EMR CD0010)

Piano Concerto in C, 2008-15
(available from EM Records, EMR CD037-8)

Symphony, 2013-15

STERNE, was THE MAN, 2013

Turning Points, 2015

HengeMusic, 2015

Acknowledgments

This book was written during my tenure as Playwright in Residence at Keble College, Oxford. When I began in that role, I wanted to make something I wouldn't have otherwise done, something that could only have happened because of the college, and I wanted it to be a project that could allow me to reorganise my thoughts about the world. This was that project, and I am deeply grateful to Jonathan Phillips, Roger Boden, Yvonne Murphy and everyone who supported my time there.

I am indebted to Mick Felton and Seren, whose enthusiasm for this project put a fire under it. Mick's support of my work has now created two books, this and my study of Peter Gill, of which I am as proud as anything I've ever written. His willingness to let me pursue this line in his livery is an extraordinary gift to a writer.

Thanks are always due to Bernard O'Donoghue, my tutor at Oxford. With the passing of years, I become ever more aware that my work is all due to his steadying hand on the tiller at a crucial moment. Over the course of this writing, I feel I have rediscovered some of what he taught me, about myself as a person as well as a writer. I must thank him, therefore, for showing me how to look.

I would also like to thank my wife, Charlie, who has helped me think through so many of the ideas in this book.

Last of all, thanks are due to Dad, for writing the music, and undertaking this exploration with me.

David Owen Norris – A Chronology

1953 – Born in Long Buckby, Northamptonshire, the younger son of Albert and Margaret Norris.

1964 – Attends Daventry Grammar School.

1972 – Elected as a Fellow of the Royal College of Organists; goes up to Oxford to read Music at Keble College, where he is appointed organ scholar.

1975 – Graduates from Oxford; studies at the Royal Academy of Music.

1977 – Studies with Yvonne Lefebure in Paris.

1978 – Works as a repetiteur at the Royal Opera House and as a harpist at the Royal Shakespeare Company.

1979 – Appointed as a Professor at the Royal Academy of Music.

1980 – Concludes his employment with the Opera House and the RSC.

1981 – Competes in the Sydney Piano Competition.

1982 – Elected as a Fellow of the Royal Academy of Music; competes in the Geneva Piano Competition.

1987 – Appointed as Artistic Director of the Petworth Festival. First son, Barnaby William Norris, born in January.

1988 – Presenter of *The Works* for BBC Radio 3.

1989 – Second son, Josiah George Norris, born in May.

1990 – Leaves his teaching role at the Academy; last broadcast of *The Works*. Presents his first television programme, *The Real Thing?*

1991 – Selected as the inaugural Gilmore Artist.

1992 – Appointed the Gresham Professor of Music, and Chairman of the Steans Institute for Singers, Chicago.

1993 – Resigns as artistic director of the Petworth Festival; appointed artistic director of the Cardiff International Festival. Presenter of In Tune, BBC Radio 3.

1996 – Leaves the Cardiff International Festival; leaves role as presenter of *In Tune*.

1997 – Concludes terms as Gresham Professor of Music and Chairman of the Steans Institute.

1998 – Appointed visiting professor at the Royal College of Music. Presents *Building a Library* for the first time, BBC Radio 3.

2000 – Appointed as an AHRC Research Fellow at the University of Southampton.

2002 – Premiere of *Think only this*, a song cycle.

2006 – Premiere of *Tomorrow Nor Yesterday*, a song cycle, and *Prayerbook*, an oratorio.

2008 – Premiere of Piano Concerto in C.

2010 – Appointed visiting professor at the Royal Northern College of Music; first broadcasts of the *Playlist* series, BBC Radio 4.

2013 – Premieres of a revised version of *Tomorrow nor Yesterday*, a Symphony, and *Sterne, was The Man*; presenter of *Chord of the Week*, BBC 2.

2015 – Premiere of revised versions of the Piano Concerto in C and the Symphony, and of *Turning Points* and *HengeMusic*. Appointed a Fellow of the Society of Antiquaries.

Index